What Others Are Sa

Barry, as usual, your scripts work! I called and asked the receptionist for the manager of a group. Got his direct number, left a message. He called back and we spoke and he asked for my resume. Thanks for your help. It does work, much to my surprise. **-Tom Wagner**
Strategic Account Manager

Barry is a certified local treasure here in Houston and with his new book, Americans everywhere will learn what we've come to know ourselves – that job searching is a fantastic opportunity for personal growth, once job seekers embrace the new habits of success he shares. As a guest speaker at our Job Ministry in The Woodlands, he always draws a strong crowd of job seekers, eager to learn and apply his techniques to accelerate their job search.
–Kevin Williams
Founder of Between Jobs Ministry/The Woodlands

I had an interview with a large firm that has been seeing people on a constant basis. I used my S.O.A.R.s as Barry taught. The GM stated that I had just been thrown the "Hail Mary Pass" and 'caught the ball!'   **-Richard Arias**

Mr. Vanek shares valuable insights and techniques to help the unemployed or those looked to advance their careers. He knows what companies want and how to market oneself right into the job of your dreams. It is because of his knowledge that I was able to land a great Job with a great salary.   **-Lisa Smith**
Vice President, Remington Support Services, Inc.

I am convinced that your *PowerNetworking* workshop and software will help me find a job, but even more importantly will help me become a better person. Thank you.
-Arnold Sherey PMP
Project Management Professional

I want to let everyone know that Barry Vanek is right. When the person interviewing you sits back, puts his hands behind his head and exposes his underarms to you...the job is yours. It actually happened to me 3 different times. The final time was when the job was offered to me. Great Teaching!　　　**-Ruben Expinoza**

Barry Vanek presents an easy to follow strategy for making effective telephone cold calls. His proven techniques for overcoming fear and hesitancy are invaluable to job seekers, consultants, and professional sales people alike.
-Bill Denning

Barry, yours is such a 'can do' upbeat message with do-able action steps. I felt motivated, uplifted, and enabled. Thank you.　　　**-Cindy Pike**

Barry's "Interviewing Techniques" advice is outstanding. I learned more in one hour than I have in months!
-Pacho Guevara

I learned a lot about interviewing from you. I had an interview yesterday and I was ready to give her my S.O.A.R.s. She was quite impressed with me, and made a lot of notes. I'm positive that I will land this one. Good job, Mr. Vanek! Thank you once again. **-Rachel Vandenberg**

Having been in sales for the last 20+ years, everything you say is spot on. I had to kick myself for some of the bad habits I've fallen into over the last year...I thank you for your reminder to do what I did for years with conviction! Thank you for your insight.　　　**–Michael Walsh**

I have known Barry Vanek for 9 years and have worked with him for 5 of those years. He is a man of much integrity, an outstanding and very organized leader, congenial, and respectful of those around him. He always has a 'can-do' attitude, and is quick to praise and reward those that work for him; a 'when I win, we all win' philosophy. I highly value Barry's opinion and have looked to him as a mentor in both my personal and professional lives.　　　**-Mike Blane**
Station Support Computer Engineer

Table of Contents

Introduction: What This Book Will Do for YOU   1
Tool #1 Looking at What You *Do*   11

- THE TELEPHONE -

Tool #2 THE Single Greatest Tool   15
Tool #3 Why We Don't Use the Phone   21
Tool #4 Replacing Fear with Courage   27
Tool #5 Whom to Call   37
Tool #6 The Daily Steps to Get a Job   47
Tool #7 Telephone Scripts   51
Tool #8 Common Responses to Calls   67

- INTERVIEW TECHNIQUES -

Tool #9 Interview Techniques Overview   71
Tool #10 Preparation   77
Tool #11 Presentation   93
Tool #12 Pacing   109
Tool #13 Topic of MONEY   123
Tool #14 Persistence   129

- POWERNETWORKING -

Tool #15 Brave New World, Brave New Rules   137
Tool #16 The *New* Job Security   141
Tool #17 Networking vs. *PowerNetworking*   147
Tool #18 S.M.A.R.T. Goals   151
Tool #19 Your Reach   163
Tool #20 Pick and Shovel Work   167
Tool #21 *Correctly* Working Your Contacts   179
Tool #22 People Skills Overview   191
Tool #23 People Skills - Your Attitude   193
Tool #24 People Skills - Meeting People   201
Tool #25 Where to Network   213
Closing Comments   217
Appendix A List of Emotions   219
Appendix B How to Create a Personal Bio   223
Appendix C *PowerNet* Software Instructions   225
Bibliography   228

About the Author

J. Barry Vanek PMP
is founder and President of **Vanek Career Services** (division of Vanek Enterprises). Mr. Vanek has 25 years in corporate America working in Fortune 500 companies. As a certified project manager, he has managed a host of large capital projects on a global scale.

He has worked with start-up companies as well as fortune 500 corporations in various capacities. His experiences include: telecommunications, oil field services, managed healthcare, consulting, international manufacturing, international construction and banking. His last position, before founding Vanek Enterprise, was as vice president of technology at JPMorgan/Chase Bank.

Mr. Vanek founded Vanek Career Services to **serve the needs of the displaced worker.** His wealth of experiences over the years has given him the insight into the needs of the displaced worker, including recent graduates as well as seasoned professionals. They all lacked the skills to *effectively* find work and manage their careers.

Mr. Vanek is a graduate of Houston Baptist University with a Bachelor of Arts in Business Management and Economics. He is an international speaker, professional orchestra conductor, and professional musician with multiple recordings to his credit.

Forward

At one time or another most *everyone* looks for a job. This is one of life's challenges. And it seems that this occurs with more and more frequency as our economy changes rapidly. The skills required to find a job and manage a career are not automatic in life. They must be learned. The sad part is that most people either *never* learn how to manage their careers or learn too late to do anything about it.

Barry has done a masterful job presenting the 'tools' necessary to not only *Get A Job...NOW!!!*, but also to manage your career from now on. The approaches are notably sound, well documented, well presented and will be an asset to everyone who chooses to follow his sound advice.

Barry has also opened a world of possibilities for those who are not looking to find a job, but rather are seeking to increase their business by increasing their reach. His teaching on *PowerNetworking* is essential to the success of anyone in life. I plan to make use of the tools myself.

You, too, will do well to take control of your life by using the tools he provides.

Jim Will, Ph.D. and Associates, Inc.
Author of *The Power of Self Talk* and *The Image Analysis Workbook*

Oxford-Hanover Publisher
(713) 622-4604
2929 Buffalo Speedway, Suite 801
Houston, TX 77098
www.jimwillphd.com

Acknowledgments

I have not attempted to cite in the text all the authorities and sources consulted in the preparation of this book. This book was the product of help from hundreds of displaced workers. These people were at an ebb in their lives wanting to go back to work. These people shared with me their tribulations, their hurts, their frustrations, and their dreams.

These people instilled in me a life changing desire to help them…. to help them get back to work and to excel in their career…. to help them truly live the 'American Dream'. It is to this end that I dedicate this book to them and for them.

No author can write a book without a great deal of support. At the top of the list is my best friend, editor, manager, and confidant, Alice Vanek, the real genius behind this work, my wife of 26 years and as I tell people, "We are still on our honeymoon". Honey…here is to another 26 years of bliss.

Finally, I wish to acknowledge my good friend, Jim Will PhD, who opened my eyes and allowed me to see my God-given potential. Without Jim, I would not have even thought this was possible. Thank you, Jim.

A Word From the Author

Getting a job has never been harder. If you have been out of work for any time at all, I do not have to tell you this. Wanting to go to work and not finding a job is very frustrating. I know. I have been where you may be.

This book is designed to give you the tools necessary to <u>Get A Job...NOW!!!</u> It will kick-start your job campaign in such a way so that you will not only find a job quickly, but also never be without work again.

I have counseled countless people who were out of work. What I have learned is that they all seem to have one thing in common: **they lack of tools necessary to find a job.** They seem to stumble from one job to another as fate dictates, but they seem to be unable to 'make it happen' on their own. Another frustrating experience.

I have focused my career on helping people <u>Get A Job...NOW!!!</u> as well as manage their careers. I know what works and what does not. I also know that the tools necessary to get a job and manage a career do not come automatically. No, they are acquired. Reading this book will give you these tools.

I pray that you apply what you learn in these pages and make your life better now, and from now on.

J. Barry Vanek PMP
Houston, TX

Disclaimer

This book is designed to provide information about the subject matter covered. It is sold with the understanding that the publisher and the authors are not engaged in rendering legal, accounting, or any other professional services expressed or implied. If these expert services are required, a competent professional should be sought.

It is not the purpose of this manual to reprint all the information that is otherwise available to authors and other creative people, but to complement, amplify and supplement other texts. For more information, see the references in the Appendix.

Finding employment is not an exact science. It is controlled entirely by humans with all of their frailties and peculiarities. This book attempts to generalize issues that may or may not help an individual. These are merely suggestions that have worked for others and may work for the reader. No guarantees are expressed or implied. Therefore, this text should only be used as a guideline and not as the absolute authority on the subject.

The disclaimer for the attached software is included in the readme.txt file.

The purpose of this handbook is to educate and entertain. The authors and SOAR Publishing shall have neither liability nor responsibility to any person or entity with respect to any loss of damage caused or alleged to be caused directly or indirectly by the information contained in this book.

If you do not wish to be bound by the above, you may return this book to the publisher for a full refund less shipping.

What This Book Will Do For YOU...

First, and foremost, this is a

Handbook for the Job Seeker.

If you are reading this, you are most likely:

- Out of work, looking for a job.
- Soon to be out of work.
- Stuck in a dead end job and wanting out.
- Wanting to change careers.
- Just starting your working career.

If any of these situations describes your situation, this book was written for YOU. It was written to help you move forward with a better job, a better career, and a better life. Lets look at how this book will get you where you want to be and get you there quickly:

- **Out of work looking for a job.**
If you are out of work, *Get A Job...NOW!!!* will give you the tools you need and instructions on how to use them. These tools will get you back to work FAST!

- **Soon to be out of work.**

If you are looking at being laid off in the near future, *Get A Job...NOW!!!* will give you the tools you need to create a 'soft landing' at a job you want.

- **Stuck in a dead end job and wanting out.**

If you are seemingly stuck in a job you hate, *Get A Job...NOW!!!* will show you how to make that dream job a reality.

- **Wanting to change careers.**

If you have worked in a career for many years and want to change directions, *Get A Job...NOW!!!* will give you the necessary steps to do just that.

- **Just starting your working career.**

Congratulations! *Get A Job...NOW!!!* will give you the tools necessary to propel and control your career from now on.

As with all handbooks, *Get A Job...NOW!!!* contains topics which may be referred to as needed. Simply find the topic with which you need direction/help/insight and turn there. Each topic's teaching is complete within itself. Of course, reading the entire book will give you the full benefit and understanding of the job-hunting process. Doing so will also greatly expedite your going back to work.

Get A Job...NOW!!! will give you the tools necessary to get back to work *quickly*. Not only that, it will also help you to excel in your career by moving up, on your terms, when you want to....and to never again be at the mercy of the "system".

After decades of helping displaced workers, I have discovered there are three root problems common among the unemployed. *Get A Job...NOW!!!* addresses these root problems:

The Root Problems. *Get A Job...NOW!!!* addresses the three root problems people have in their job search and career advancement:

1. How to use the telephone in order to get the interview.
2. How to interview so as to distinguish yourself from your competition.
3. How to network with the expressed purpose of advancing your career.

Knowing how to effectively overcome these problems will get you back to work *quickly*.

If you are 18 and looking for your first job or 55 and looking to change your career, you NEED THIS BOOK. It will make your dream job a reality. It has for countless others and it will for you.

"A craftsman is only as good as the tools in his toolbox"
-Tim 'The Toolman' Taylor

Central Theme of
Get A Job...NOW!!!

'Tools' is the theme of Get A Job...NOW!!!; the 'tools' necessary to move forward in your job campaign and career. The chapters are actually entitled 'Tools', and rightly so. When used properly, each 'Tool' will help you become a skilled craftsman who knows how to 'make things happen' and get you back to work NOW!!!

To highlight each tool, there will be a familiar icon, , a blade screwdriver. This will alert you to the tool and its use. After understanding how the tool is to be used, use it to its fullest.

This book is divided into three sections:
- The Telephone - THE Single Greatest Tool.
- Interviewing Techniques - How to Distinguish Yourself.
- *PowerNetworking* - The *New* Job Security

THE Telephone - The Single Greatest Tool. How to *effectively* use the phone will give you the tools necessary to find decision makers. It will show you the power at your disposal and how to take advantage of it. If you are afraid of using the phone, you will learn how to replace fear with courage using a technique called 'supersedence'. It will teach you how to locate decision makers and get the appointments.

Interview Techniques – How to Distinguish Yourself. Next, you will be given the tools necessary to distinguish yourself in the interview process. You will learn how to make that all-important first impression, how to endear the decision maker to you as a person, and how to make him 'feel good about you'.

PowerNetworking – **The** *New* **Job Security.** Lastly, you will learn how to propel your career with *PowerNetworking*. You will grab the power at your disposal and become an important part of people's lives; people who can help you become a success. This is *real* job security. And it is yours, if you learn how to make it a reality.

Get A Job...NOW!!! will give you 25 tools for your 'Job Campaign' toolbox. These tools will make you a powerhouse at finding work and securing your career for as long as you wish to work.

The topics covered are:

Tool #1 Looking at What You *Do..* What we 'do' determines what happens to us. This tool exposes the reality that you *can* change what is happening to you by changing what you 'do'. We explore just how vital it is to determine to change what you are doing and start doing those things that will get you a job.

Page...........11

THE TELEPHONE includes Tools #2 – 8:

Tool #2 THE Single Greatest Tool. The telephone brings with it the power that can get you back to work quickly and advance your career. We explore the power at your disposal and its ability to insure your success in the job market.   Page.........15

Tool #3 Why We Don't Use the Phone. Understanding why we are afraid of using the phone is the first step in being able to use the phone effectively. This tool explores the root causes of why we are afraid of using the phone.   Page.........21

Tool #4 Replacing Fear with Courage. It is not enough to just 'not be afraid' to pick up the phone. No, you must have courage to pick up the phone and make the calls necessary to get a job. This tool will enable you to supersede fear with courage. It discusses a technique called 'supersedence', which links the emotional state of courage to a physical stimulus.
                    Page.........27

Tool #5 Whom to Call. This tool will show you how to make vertical marketing lists. It will show you the two main lists of people you should contact. You will be given the necessary forms to use in tracking your calls so that when people call back, you will not have to count on your memory to know whom they are.
                    Page.........37

Tool #6 The Daily Steps to Get a Job. There are some people who do not know what to do on a day-to-day basis to get a job. Nothing they have tried has worked. If this is you, this list is especially for you. It will order your steps on a daily basis so that you can move forward to quickly find work.   Page.........47

Tool #7 Telephone Scripts. All professionals use scripts. The scripts will free you to concentrate on getting the face-to-face interview. These scripts are designed to locate the decision makers and get the interview.   Page..........51

Tool #8 Common Responses to Calls. As you begin your telephone campaign, you will receive various responses.   This tool gives you the necessary comebacks to common responses.   Page.........67

INTERVIEW TECHNIQUES includes Tools # 9 – 14:

Tool #9 Interview Techniques Overview. During the interview process people are included or excluded. This tool gives you an overview of the entire interview process and how important it is.   Read this before reading the following tools, which cover the various details of this process.   Page.........71

Tool #10 Preparation.   Being prepared for the interview is essential to your getting the job. This tool explores how to investigate the company BEFORE you get in front of the decision maker.   Knowing key information about the company and decision makers will make you 'look smart'.   Page.........77

Tool # 11 Presentation. How we look determines how we are received. This tool teaches you how to not be *'Green Eggs and Ham'*. It explores the topic of dressing for success, what to wear and what not to wear, and what is appropriate and what is not. You never get a second chance to make a first impression. This tool assures you of a good first impression. Page..........93

Tool #12 Pacing. There are techniques designed to place the other person 'at ease' with you as a person.

This tool teaches you how to make people 'feel good about you'. Body language, theirs and yours, will make you a 'Member of Their Tribe." Page........109

Tool #13 Topic of Money. At some point the topic of money is discussed. How you approach it and how you avoid it can mean the difference between getting what you want and leaving money on the table. These simple techniques will assure you of going into the job with the greatest income. Page........123

Tool #14 Persistence. After you leave the interview, what can you do to gain an edge on your competition? This tool gives you suggestions on what to do post-interview. It even instructs you on how to benefit from the interview even if you did not get the position.
Page........129

POWERNETWORKING includes Tools # 14 – 25:

Tool #15 Brave New World, Brave New Rules. In this 'Brave New World', is there such a thing as real job security? Not in the traditional sense because the rules have changed. If you know the new rules you can have job security. This tool will give you the security everyone wants. Page........137

Tool #16 The New Job Security. There is a way to be secure in your career; to never be without work. Having this security requires knowing how to create it for yourself. This tool will explain how to have real job security. Page........141

Tool #17 Networking vs. *PowerNetworking*. There is a huge difference between meeting a lot of people and having a *PowerNetwork*. This tool will teach you how to turn your meaningless list of names into a

PowerNetwork. This *PowerNetwork* will insure your success now and throughout your career.

Page........147

Tool #18 S.M.A.R.T. Goals. Setting goals in life can either frustrate us or propel us. Knowing how to set S.M.A.R.T. goals is the difference. This tool will make your dreams come true in your job search as well as any other area of life. Page........151

Tool #19 Your Reach. It has been said, 'It is not what you know but whom you know'. This tool explores the number of people who are at your disposal and how to reach them. Page........163

Tool #20 Pick and Shovel Work. In order to convert your network into a *PowerNetwork*, you must have a system. This tool is that system. It includes a paper based system as well as an introduction to the software program *PowerNet*, which is included with this book. It is a powerful program designed specifically for one purpose: to create and maintain your *PowerNetwork*.

Page........167

Tool #21 *Correctly* Working Your Contacts. This tool explores how to make logical connections within your network for the purpose of creating *PowerNetwork* contacts. The 'connect-the-dots' approach will add value to each of your contacts. This added value will endear them to you as a person. Page........179

Tool #22 People Skills Overview. This tool introduces Tools #23 – 24 dealing with people skills. Understanding how each people-skill tool functions is important, so read about this tool before reading the others. Page........191

Tool #23 People Skills - Your Attitude. Your attitude determines a host of issues in your life. Getting a job is one of those issues. This tool will teach you how to defeat a negative attitude by replacing it with a positive attitude. Page........193

Tool #24 People Skills - Meeting People. Meeting strangers is hard for some people. Knowing how to initiate 'small talk' designed to 'break the ice' is what this tool teaches. These proven methods will make you comfortable meeting strangers. Done properly, it even becomes fun. Page........201

Tool #25 Where to Network. There are several types of networking events. This tool explores how to be effective at each; to be able to make key contacts that can get you a job and/or propel your career.
Page........213

Closing Comments. This section gives instructions on how to obtain various training videos and books to help you in your search. This is a listing of resources that are designed to help the displaced worker.
Page........217

Appendix A is a list of emotions.

Page.........219

Appendix B has information on how to create a personal bio along with several examples.
Page........223

Appendix C contains a set of *PowerNet* software instructions. Page........225

Bibliography. Listed here are additional books on the topics contained in this book. Page........228

Order forms for additional materials Page........230

Looking at What You DO...

What you *do* determines...
what happens to you.

This is a statement of fact. What comes our way is a direct result of the choices we make. What we choose to do on a moment-by-moment, day-by-day basis determines what happens to us. Wise choices bring positive results and unwise choices bring negative results. It is just that simple.

Knowing this simple fact frees you to change; to change what you are doing that is *not* working in order to do what *will* work. In other works, to produce the results you desire. In this case, *Get A Job...NOW!!!*

"He that will not apply new remedies must expect new evils."
- Bacon (1561-1626)

You must decide to change if you want to move forward with your job search or your career advancement. *You must* make the conscious decision to make changes that will move you forward.

Fortunately, the 'what to do' is detailed in this book. Your reading this book indicates your willingness to make those changes. To *do* the things that will get you the interviews and to meet the people necessary to get the results you desire.

To reinforce this, lets look at an observable truth of life:

The Rich get richer...
and the poor get poorer.

We have all heard this phrase. And we believe it to be true. We believe it to be true because history tells us it is true. But *why* is this true? Why do the rich continue to get richer and the poor continue to get poorer? The answer is simple:

**"Because the rich *DO* what the rich *DO*...
and the poor *DO* what the poor *DO*!!!**

So the first tool in your tool box is the realization that:

"Changing what you *do*, will change what will happen to you."

Stated another way:

> *To be a success,*
> > *do what successful people do!*

<u>**Looking at What You *Do...***</u>

The choice is yours. It is very important for you to realize that you *can* decide to change what you are doing. You *can* decide to do things differently. You *can* decide to stop what is not working. You *can* make these choices.

Sad fact. Most people do not like to change what they are doing, even if it is wrong. They understand that what they are doing is not producing the desired results. They know that what they are doing is not working. But they continue to do the same things over and over again. And they receive the same failing results over and over again. So how do you break this cycle of non-productive behavior? You must do two things:

1. You must make the following confession:

"What I am doing is not working. *I will* learn what *does* work and *do it!*"

This simple statement will free you to succeed. Free you to learn what to do to get a job. Free you to learn new techniques, new approaches, and new attitudes that will insure your success.

"We can do anything we want to do if we stick to it long enough."
                                               - Helen Keller (1880-1968)

2. Immediately stop non-productive behavior!
It is imperative that you stop doing what is not

working. It should be no mystery to you what is not working. You are doing it every day. So stop it now.

> For example, I had a client who was highly educated and extremely qualified in his field. He told me, "I have sent out over 1000 resumes on the Internet and still do not have a job."

What does this tell you? **Sending resumes on the Internet did not work for him!!!**

Hard to face the truth. Now, this admission is not an easy thing to do. No, to tell ourselves that what we are doing is wrong takes courage. It is much easier to hide behind our pride and say, "we are so good at what we do that the world will beat a path to our door". The only problem is that the world is not beating a path to your door, is it?

"It is impossible for a man to learn what he thinks he already knows."
-Epictetus (50-138 A.D.)

Finally, realize that what you *do* determines what *happens to you* AND that you, and you alone, can make the difference. You *can* make things happen. You *are* in control. You *will* be able to get the perfect job. You *are not* at the mercy of 'the system'. You *can* make things better for you and your family. You *can* have security.

"To live is to change, and to be perfect is to have changed often."
-John Henry Newman (1801-1890)

THE TELEPHONE, THE Single Greatest Tool

The single most important concept you can learn from this book is this one simple truth:

"The telephone is THE greatest tool the displaced worker has."

Why is the telephone so important to the displaced worker? To answer this, lets first explore the *power* of the telephone:

The Power of the Telephone. In a single 2 hour period, you can easily make 24 phone calls (if each call takes 5 minutes). That totals:

* 120 contacts per week.

* 500 contacts per month.

*6000 contacts per year.

Now, ask yourself the question, "Is there someone in those 500 phone calls me make in a month that can help me secure a job?" The answer, of course, is:

YES!!!

Ask yourself another question: "Is this power at my disposal to use?" Again, the answer is:

YES!!!

OK, lets take it a step further. Lets say you made calls for 4 hours each day and called 48 people. That totals:

*240 contacts per week.

*1000 contacts per month.

*12,000 contacts per year.

Don't just read past those numbers. Look at them. You are talking about people who can potentially put you to work; people who will help you when you ask for help; people who will put you in contact with those who can get you your next job. In addition, you are developing contacts that can give you the inside track on the jobs that no one else knows about. This power is at your disposal: power to make contact with 100's of decision makers WITHOUT LEAVING YOUR HOME...

Advantage in the market. This power, to contact 'targeted' individuals, will give you the 'hands up' advantage over those who simply look at the want ads...or those who search the net...or those who fill out endless application forms.

Effectively using the telephone will make the difference in your being employed or unemployed... now and in the future.

It is a numbers game.

When using the telephone, understand that it is a numbers game. In a numbers game, the winners are those with the greatest numbers. Let me illustrate:

> At Vanek Career Services, each day we:
> - Make 50 phone calls.
> - Talk to between 10 and 25 people.
> - Leave 10 and 25 voice messages.
> - And, most importantly:
>   **Make 1 appointment with a decision maker!!!**

How to make the numbers work for you. The numbers can be put to work for you...*but* understand that there is only one person who can do it. There is only one person who determines the number of calls you make each day...YOU. *You* decide if you want the numbers to work for you or against you. *You* and you alone are responsible for making the calls. No one else. Just you.

This fact is both good news and bad news.
- Good news because you now know that you can control the number of calls you make.
- Bad news because you now know that you can control the number of calls you make.

The ball is in your court. It is up to you. And you CAN DO IT.

Fear of using the phone. To most people, using the telephone is not what they want to do. They are afraid of using the phone. In Tool #4, you will be given the tools necessary to replace the 'fear of using the phone' with 'courage to use the phone'. In Tool #5, you will learn what to say to find decision makers and get the appointment. So hang in there, there is a lot more to come.

But, first things first: in order for you to move forward, you need to *decide* to move forward. You must make a quality decision to learn to use the phone. Lets explore the power of a quality decision...

Quality decision

A quality decision will mean the difference in your success or failure. The operative word is *Quality*. Most people in life do not want to make quality decisions. They don't make these decisions because it calls them to *action*.   It holds them accountable for moving forward to act out their decision.

Failures already. Those who do not make quality decisions are already failures.   Read the following quote from President Theodore Roosevelt:

"The credit belongs to the man who is actually in the arena; whose face is marred by dust and sweat and blood; who strives valiantly; who knows the great enthusiasms, the great devotions, and spends himself in a worthy cause; who at the best knows in the end the triumph of high achievement; and who at the worst, if he fails, at least fails while daring greatly…"

-Theodore Roosevelt (1859-1919)
26th President of the United States

Theodore Roosevelt had severe asthma as a child. He was hyperactive and apparently suffered from attention deficit. He was a sickly child who suffered from frequent incidences of diarrhea and colds. To combat his poor physical condition, his father urged him to take up exercise at a local gym. After a couple of beatings from his peers, Theodore took up boxing as a sport. Theodore made the **quality decision** to beat his illness, to do better, to get in the fight, to strive for excellence in spite of physical or mental restraints. He never gave into failure. He saw every defeat as a victory by having been in the arena of life. And as long as he had breath, he would keep up the fight. He would go on to become the 26th President of the United States and, at the age of 42, the youngest President we have ever had. As a postscript: a book was found under his pillow on his deathbed. He was making himself better up to the very end…

Now is the time to make the quality decision that will change your life. It is time to put aside all former failures, mistakes and frustrations that are preventing you from moving forward. It is time to put a stake in the ground that says, '*Today*, I have decided *I am* going to learn what I do not know. *I am* going to learn what it takes to be a success. *I am* going to learn how to move forward in my job search and take charge of my career……no matter what!!!"

"It does not take much strength to do things, but it requires great strength to decide on what to do."
-Elbert Hubbard (1859-1915)
American author and publisher

Theodore Roosevelt

"The unforgivable crime is soft hitting.
Do not hit at all if it can be avoided;
But, never hit softly."
-Theodore Roosevelt (1858-1919)
26th President of the United States

Why We Don't Use The Phone

Why don't you make the calls necessary to get a job? If the telephone is the most effective tool to use in your job search (and it is…), why don't you use the phone effectively in your job campaign? In this chapter, we will explore the reasons we don't use the telephone. Then Tool #4 will give us the tools to overcome these challenges.

Reasons for not using the telephone:
1. Pride
2. Fear

Pride. The first reason people do not use the phone is pride. If you have an issue with pride, I am sorry to say that I cannot help you. It has been written:

"Pride goes before destruction and a haughty spirit before a fall."

-King Solomon of Israel 900 BC

Pride has many faces that will cause you ruin:

- Pride will cause an attitude of self-sufficiency and you won't take another's advice.
- Pride will stop all forward motion in your job search.
- Pride will tell you that you are 'too good' to *lower* yourself to calling and asking for help.
- Pride will tell you that you are so good that the world will beat a path to your door.
- Pride will feed on itself to the point that depression will eventually take over because of your lack of employment.

"In general, pride is at the bottom of all great mistakes."
-John Ruskin (1819-1900)
English critic and theorist

Pride is not a pretty sight and the solution can only come from within *you*. Only you can humble yourself. Doing so will enable you to move forward and quickly propel your job search and/or career. Humbling yourself will cause doors to open that you will easily walk through. It has also been written:

"Humble yourself under the mighty hand of God and He will exalt you in due time."
-Saint Peter (6 BC-40 AD?)

Fear. The second reason people do not use the telephone is fear. The good news is that there is help available for the problem of fear…

"For it is not death or hardship that is a fearful thing, but the *fear* of death and hardship."

-Epictetus (50-138 A.D.)
Phrygian philosopher

What people fear about using the telephone.

First, people are afraid of rejection. There are few things in life that are as demeaning as being fired or laid off from a job. Being told that you are not wanted any more causes emotional pain at all levels. Why is this?

In America, we tend to place much of our self-worth in our jobs. We often feel that 'who we are' is defined by 'what we do'. When we are not wanted any more at our job, we feel as if our value as a person is somehow diminished. This is often followed by emotions of guilt, fright, anxiety, anger and a host of other negative emotions. These emotions can eventually lead to depression and associated physical illness.

'The fear of further rejection is to be avoided at all costs' is the mantra of the wounded soul. This mantra will prevent a person from making the phone calls necessary to get a job.

Second, people are afraid of stepping into the unknown. People do not make the phone calls necessary to get a job because it is stepping into unfamiliar territory. It is scary to venture where you have not been before. Using the telephone requires stepping off the edge of the 'familiar and comfortable' into the abyss of the dark and foreboding territory of 'strangers'. And we all remember our mothers warning us, "...don't speak to strangers!"

Third, people are afraid of getting out of their 'comfort zone.' The familiar job, with its familiar people, familiar surroundings, familiar bosses, and familiar income had a great deal of comfort...like an old pair of shoes. They may not look all that great, but they are comfortable. We have learned to live with them, no matter how bad they look or feel. Using the phone to look for work is like breaking in a new pair of shoes. We think it will be painful and wrought with distress...in short, uncomfortable. And we do NOT want to be uncomfortable.

"The ultimate measure of a man is not where he stands in moments of comfort and convenience, but where he stands at times of challenge and controversy."
                              -Martin Luther King, Jr. (1929-1968)
                              Civil rights leader and clergyman

Finally, people are afraid of failing AGAIN!!!! Losing a job can be perceived as failing. It is very easy to look in the mirror and tell yourself you are a failure, "If you were not a failure, you would not have lost your job." Picking up the phone to be rejected again would only reinforce your thinking that you are a failure. The last thing you want to do is to knowingly put yourself in a position to fail again.

These fears are real and to deny they exist is foolish. These real fears will prevent you from making the phone calls necessary to get your job.

But, understand that these fears can be replaced with courage. Tool #4 will teach you how you can do this.

"Fear is the darkroom where negatives are developed"
                                        -George Clue (1927-2002)

"Depression, gloom, pessimism, despair, discouragement, these slay ten human beings to every one murdered by typhoid, influenza, diabetes or pneumonia. If tuberculosis is the great white plague, then *fear* is the great black plague."
                                        -Gilbert Murray (1866-1957)
                                        English classical scholar

Replacing Fear with Courage

Courage. **What is it?** Lets talk about courage. The truth is, you can do anything if you are not afraid. Remember when you were 5 years old. You thought anything was possible. You would attempt anything with no regard for 'life or limb.' For some, this does not stop when they turn 6. It continues through young adulthood.

There is a medical term used in emergency rooms to describe certain injuries. The term is "YMIS," pronounced Y'mis. It stands for 'young man's invincibility syndrome'. YMIS describes a 19-year-old male who did something foolhardy and got injured, such as hiking the Grand Canyon in flip-flops with no water (a guaranteed formula for a trip to the hospital). Or a motocross rider who refused to wear protective equipment and received multiple broken bones. Or a downhill skier who attempted to conquer the black slopes with 'bunny' slope skills. When the emergency room triage nurse determines the injury and decides it is caused from a 'big case of the *stupids*...' it is termed "YMIS." The point to be made here is that courage will enable you to do things you would not *normally* do.

Courage is the key. Courage is the key to effective use of the telephone. With courage, you will achieve the unimaginable. You will make the calls and locate key decision makers. You will meet key people. You will discover new opportunities. You will propel your career like you never dreamed possible.

Fear must be replaced. It is important to note that it is not enough to just "not be afraid." No, you must *have courage*. You must replace fear with courage to effectively use the telephone.

So how do you replace fear with courage?

Before learning how to replace fear with courage, you need to understand something about fear. Fear is an emotion. To understand fear better, you must first know what an emotion is:

Definition of "emotion":
      Noun; positive or negative feelings generally in reaction to stimuli (real or imagined) that are accompanied by physiological arousal and related behavior.

      Emotions are feelings. Here are a few emotions with which you can easily identify: Fear, Anger, Hate, Joy, Love, Anxiety, Courage, Loneliness, Boredom.
See Appendix A for a more extensive list of emotions.

      Each of these emotions can be generated by real or imagined events. But either way, they can be *replaced*.

Replacing one emotion for another.

Notice the operative word is *replaced*. Emotions can be replaced. It is possible to replace one emotion with another. You understand this principle. For example: It is possible to replace the emotion of loneliness with happiness. People do it by going to the movies. Some people 'get lost' in the emotions of a romance novel or action book. Comic books, music, hobbies...all are designed to replace a negative emotion with a positive one. So, you now understand that *emotions can be replaced*. Perhaps the better word for replacing one emotion for another is to **supersede** one emotion with another emotion.

The Technique:
"Supersedence."

There is a technique called *"Supersedence."* This is **the act of superseding (replacing) one emotional state with another.** With this tool, you will be able to supersede fear with courage. Furthermore, with *supersedence*, you will be able to "fill your soul with courage" whenever or wherever you want, or need it. This means that courage is at your disposal to replace fear so that you can make the phone calls, interview like a professional and create a power network that will insure your success.

You will now learn the technique of *supersedence.* Before we start, let me encourage you to make the *quality decision* to do the following *exercise* exactly as described. I assure you that you will find the experience enjoyable. You will find it liberating. Some have even found it to be life changing. You will come to use this tool with great effectiveness not only in your job search, but in other areas of your life as well. I also encourage you to make the *quality decision* to do this exercise twice daily for 7 days straight. If you miss a day, the 7 days begin again. Done properly, this exercise will take you from two to three minutes each time. Done properly, you will look forward to the experience and master the art of *supersedence* to your benefit.

OK, let us begin...you will now learn how to supersede fear with courage.

Supersedence Exercise:

Step 1. Find a quiet place free from distractions. If the radio or TV is playing, turn it off. If there are people in the room, ask them to leave for the next 3 minutes. If you can, dim the lights. You must create a distraction-free environment.

Step 2. Find a comfortable sitting position with feet flat on the floor, hands on your legs.

Step 3. Close your eyes.

Step 4. You are now going to relax by breathing slowly and deeply 3 times. Each time, concentrate on breathing in through your nose and exhaling through your mouth. Each time you breathe in, breathe in fully to expand your lungs, hold it for a few moments and slowly breathe out through your mouth. As you do, visualize the tension leaving your body with your exhaled breath. Concentrate on feeling your arms, legs and back relax as you breathe.

After the third round of breathing, you should be totally relaxed. Don't rush this. Relaxing is a crucial step in the process.

Step 5. Now, remember a time in your life when you felt really strong... a time in your life when you were *really* in control...really powerful over all of life. This could be when you were a child hitting the big home run. Or a student receiving that 'special' award. Or an employee bringing in the 'big deal'. Go back to that time and relive it. This is your memory, so relive it once again. Everyone has experiences like these. So force yourself to recall a moment of triumph in your life.

Once you recall the event, force yourself to recall as many details as you can. Ask yourself these questions:
  * Who was there?
  * What were their names?
  * What was the weather like?
  * What clothes did I have on?

This is your memory, so lavish once again in how it felt to be strong, powerful and in control. Do not hurry this, lavish in the emotions, the feelings, the absolute joy of being there.

Step 6. With your eyes still closed, hold out your right hand with your thumb up. Next, grab your right thumb with your left hand and squeeze as hard as you can. At this moment, you should have the emotion of courage pumping through your soul and the physical sensation of both holding your thumb *and* having your thumb being squeezed...all at the same time.

Step 7. You are now going to ask yourself this question out loud, "How do I feel at this very moment?"

Step 8. Answer yourself. If you have done the process correctly, you will say, "GREAT!!!"

What you have just experienced is the technique *"supersedence."*

Very Important!!! What you have just learned *must* be repeated *twice* each day for 7 days, morning and evening. Done properly, this will take you between two and four minutes.

Now, be prepared; if you 'do' your *supersedence* exercise exactly as described, you are in store for several treats:

- Each time you "do" your *supersedence* exercise, the image will become more vivid.
- You will recall new details of the event.
- The emotion of courage will become more vivid.
- The experience will become more enjoyable, more pleasurable and more powerful.
- You will begin to experience an increase in your positive self-image.
- You will hold your shoulders a little straighter.
- You will hold your head a little higher.
- You will notice a confidence in your voice.

These are all natural side effects of properly executed *supersedence*.

Emotional courage. *Supersedence* enables you to drive an emotional stake in the ground that declares, 'I have courage and I can do *anything!!!*'

The Power of *Supersedence*

Here is the miracle of the human mind: after you have developed this *courage stake* through the act of *supersedence*, you need only grab your thumb, and the emotion of courage will *automatically flood your soul,*

and *courage replaces fear.*

"Courage and perseverance have a magical talisman, before which difficulties disappear and obstacles vanish into air."
-John Quincy Adams (1767-1848)
6th President of the United States

Supersedence is like putting an air hose to a flat tire. The tire quickly fills with air. Think of your thumb as the tire valve and your hand as the air hose that *fills your soul with courage.* When you grab your thumb, fear will leave because **courage supersedes fear**...just as surely as light replaces darkness.

If you are the doubting type that does not believe this works, understand that the Russian physiologist Ivan Petrovich Pavlov discovered the basis of this technique. Pavlov won the Nobel Peace Price for Medicine in 1904 for his pioneering work on what we now call 'classic conditioning'. A summary in technical terms of his research states:

Experiments carried out by Pavlov and his pupils showed that conditioned reflexes originate in the cerebral cortex, which acts as the prime distributor and organizer of all activity of the organism and which is responsible for the very delicate equilibrium of an animal with its environment... it was established that any external agent could, by coinciding in time with an ordinary reflex, become the conditioned signal for the formation of a new conditioned reflex.

(source: www.nobelprize.org)

How do you make *supersedence* work for you?

Quite simply:
- Grab your thumb and squeeze any time you feel fearful.
- Grab your thumb and squeeze any time you need courage to do something you know will take you out of your comfort zone.
- Grab your thumb and squeeze any time you begin to feel anxious about a situation.
- Grab your thumb and squeeze any time you are not sure about what to do next.

At these moments, when you need to supersede fear with courage, grab you thumb and squeeze... And fear WILL LEAVE. At the moment you feel the courage rising within you, move forward with whatever you know needs to be done... like:
- Making the next phone call.
- Going to the next appointment.
- Going into the room for the interview.

Remember that **after diligent application of this process,** you need only to grab your thumb and the emotion of courage will... AUTOMATICALLY FLOOD YOUR EMOTIONS!

A final word on dealing with fear.

Supersedence is a proven method to replace fear with courage. It works very well. Those who use this tool to its full effectiveness experience a secondary phenomenon: once they overcome their fear of a particular event in life that causes them so much anxiety, the actual event became less and less fearful. In fact, it eventually became a non-issue. A familiar example of this is a child's fear of the dark. All children are afraid of the dark at some point in their lives. But as they mature, they overcome that fear so that most normal people have no morbid fear of darkness. It is no longer a thought. Because facing our fears causes them to go away.

"I count him braver who overcomes his desires than him who conquers his enemies; for the hardest victory is over self."
-Aristotle (BC 384-322)

Tool #5

Whom to Call

OK, now you have a clear understanding of the power of the telephone and you have the tools necessary to replace fear with courage, so you are ready to start making the calls.

So whom do you call??? There are actually 2 groups of individuals you will be calling: friends (including family) and companies for whom you potentially want to work. We will cover each separately.

1. Lists of friends and family. Understand first and foremost, **the more people who know you are looking for work, the better.** The best approach is to start listing all of the people you know. This includes *all*. On the average, each person knows between 130 and 250 people (233 people is the average). So start by listing all 200+ people. You may say, "I do not know 200 people." **YES, YOU DO!!!**

> The average American knows 233 people.

In order to help you systematically list all of these people, there is a form called *PowerNetworking* (Figure 5A). You may duplicate this form on a word processor or copy it from this book on a copy machine that will enlarge.

You will list one person per page and file alphabetically by last name. (The software program *PowerNet*, which is included with this book, automates this process). To speed the process, organize your list by logical groupings of people. For example:

- **Family:** The first major group is your family, both close relatives and distant relatives. List each and his/her relationship to you.
- **Neighbors:** This list will include any neighbors, current as well as past.
- **Schools:** Make a list of people you know from school, including high school, college, tech school...all the people you met while in school. This is where you will include any societies, clubs or fraternities/sororities.
- **Business Contacts:** Divide these between customers, vendors, and colleagues/co-workers. Dividing your business cards into 3 stacks most easily does this.
- **Not for Profit:** These are the people you know from church, civic clubs, social clubs, country clubs, volunteer work and the like. If you can obtain a directory of members, get it and highlight the people you know.
- **Personal services:** These are the persons you know who serve you at restaurants, work on your car, clean your clothes, do your housework, sell you insurance, paint your house, do your lawn. I think you get the picture.

Note – As an added bonus, once you complete these lists, you will have an accurate up-to-date address book that will serve you well.

2. List of companies to canvas. Next, you are going to make a list of companies to canvas in your telephone campaign.

So how do you get a list of companies? A good place to start is the public library. The library has a host of books listing companies that potentially could hire you. They also have Internet access to various databases, which you can access from your home. In most cities, all you need is a library card to access their computer network. Cost is free in most cases.

When you go the library, ask the librarian for her help. Simply tell her that you are looking for work and need to be shown the various lists of companies so that you can contact them. She will show you various books and publications showing companies that meet your needs. She will also show you how to access the various databases to which the library subscribes.

Another source of company listings is the Internet. The problem here is 'you get what you pay for'. If it is free, do not expect it to be accurate or up-to-date. On the other hand, you can purchase company data from companies, like Dunn & Bradstreet, which give accurate company data including company officers and their contact information. One such web site is www.zapdata.com. This site is controlled by Dunn & Bradstreet. You purchase the number of records you want according to any number of criteria. You can purchase as few or as many records as you need. The cost is very reasonable and ranges from approximately $0.15 - $1.60 per record, depending on the amount of information you need on each company.

When you compile your list, concentrate on those companies that can most readily use your talents. For instance, if you have spent five years in sporting goods retail sales, you would want to get a listing of the sporting goods retail stores in your area of town. If you worked in a refinery as an operator, you would want to find a list of all the refineries.

Vertical Marketing. Another source of company names is the local Yellow Pages. This lists each company in logical groupings of industry. Finding logical listings of companies is termed 'vertical marketing'. This means the companies you list are all in the same industry. You will usually look for companies, which are similar to the company you last worked for.

Keeping track of phone activity. Just having a list of companies will do you no good if you do not have an effective way of keeping track of your phone activity. To make life easy on you (and we do want an easy life...) we have created a form, which has been proven to streamline your phone activity. The form is called the 'Job Communications Log Sheet'. (Figure 5B) It is also listed on our website www.GetAJob.ws/forms.

This form is a very important tool in your job search. It will keep you organized as you start and continue your job campaign. Why is this so important?

Only keep track of 7 things. Research has proven that the human mind can keep track of about 7 events. With adequate rest and a minimum of distractions, the average person can remember and attend to 7 different things during the day. This means that without a support mechanism, event #8 most likely will be forgotten or, if it is attended to, one of the original 7 items is forgotten. To solve this problem, we devote things to writing. The familiar 'to do list' is an example.

A lot of calls. When you begin your phone campaign you will be making a lot of calls. You will need to keep track of hundreds of calls and document the people with whom you spoke. You cannot just haphazardly approach your calling lists. You MUST have a system that will assure that you will not miss any calls or appointments, or forget names or important facts. The 'Job Communications Log Sheet' (Figure 5B) is the answer.

PowerNetworking

First name_____**Last name**_____[ ]Mr.[ ]Mrs.[ ]Ms.
Company Name_____ _____
Title/function_____ Birthday___/___/_____
                    Contact every [ ]30 days [ ]60 days [ ]90 days [ ]120 days [ ]Yearly

Address:
[ ]Personal [ ]Business [ ]_____   Business card
Street_____
City _____State____Zip_____
[ ]Personal [ ]Business [ ]_____
Street_____
City _____State____Zip_____
[ ]Personal [ ]Business [ ]_____
Street_____
City _____State____Zip_____

Phone (___)____-_____[ ]Home [ ]Bus. [ ]Fax [ ]Cell
Phone (___)____-_____[ ]Home [ ]Bus. [ ]Fax [ ]Cell
Phone (___)____-_____[ ]Home [ ]Bus. [ ]Fax [ ]Cell
Phone (___)____-_____[ ]Home [ ]Bus. [ ]Fax [ ]Cell

Email:
_____@_____.____[ ]Personal [ ]Bus.
_____@_____.____[ ]Personal [ ]Bus.
_____@_____.____[ ]Personal [ ]Bus.
_____@_____.____[ ]Personal [ ]Bus.

Identity:
Who they **are**_____

What they **do** _____

What they **like**_____

Figure 5A

Job Campaign Communications Log

Company name _____ Phone _____

Address _____ Fax_____

City/St _____ Website _____

Current notes on the company:_____
_____

Decision makers:

Name	Title	Phone	Email	Misc

Communications log:

Date   Spoke to   Action/information/directive/follow up

__/___ _____
__/___ _____
__/___ _____
__/___ _____
__/___ _____
__/___ _____
__/___ _____
__/___ _____
__/___ _____
__/___ _____
__/___ _____
__/___ _____
__/___ _____
__/___ _____
__/___ _____
__/___ _____
__/___ _____
__/___ _____

Figure5B

Lets take a close look at the form:

Job Campaign Communications Log

Company name_____ Phone _____
Address _____ Fax_____
City/St _____Website _____
Current notes on the company:_____
_____
_____
_____

The top of the form has the *Company name* or contact name and all contact information. You will list one company per form. After you make the initial call, you will file this form in a notebook in alphabetical order according to the company name.

The form also has a section titled *Current notes on the company*. This is where you list important information that will make you look 'smart' when you make your calls. For example: If you read that the company has just been awarded a contract for doing roofing at 3 major locations, this is where you would place this information. The company's website is a good source.

Decision makers:

Name	Title	Phone	Email	Misc

Next, is a running list of the *Decision makers* within the company. You will use this when you 'drop names'. This is where you will list the names of everyone you spoke with, starting with the receptionist. The idea is to be able to 'drop' the name of someone who works there. Each time you speak with someone, list their name and, if you can, their position within the company. You will refer to this list frequently.

Communications log:
Date   Spoke to   Action/information/directive/follow up
__/__ _____ _____
__/__ _____ _____
__/__ _____ _____
__/__ _____ _____
__/__ _____ _____
__/__ _____ _____
__/__ _____ _____
__/__ _____ _____
__/__ _____ _____
__/__ _____ _____
__/__ _____ _____

The last section is titled *Communications log* and it shows when you called and with whom you spoke. Each time you have a conversation, document it.

Why is this so important? As time goes on, you will be receiving calls from people you do not remember. When they call you back, they will generally tell you what company they are with and you can quickly find this sheet in your notebook. You will immediately see when you spoke with them and what you discussed. It keeps you from looking foolish. Also, this sheet becomes invaluable to you for on-going networking efforts. (We discuss this in the section on *PowerNetworking*.)

"Science is organized knowledge."
-Herbert Spencer (1820-1903)
English philosopher

"The secret of all victory lies in the organization of the non-obvious."
-Spengler (1880-1936)
German Philosopher

The Daily Steps to Get a Job

I have a personal story to tell you:

22 years ago, I had been married for 2 years and was having serious financial problems. My problem was I could not support my family despite our combined incomes including my 2 jobs. In today's dollars, we were spending $600 more each month than we earned. At this point, I experienced what I call an "emotional breakdown." By this I mean that I became unable to make any decisions because all my *previous* decisions had been wrong. I was desperate. As an answer to prayer, I found out about a ministry in a local church called 'Financial Freedom Seminar'. This 20 hours of training taught people how to get out of debt and stay out of debt.

I purposed to go to the seminar and do everything they said to do, whether I understood it or not. You see, I no longer had any faith in my own abilities to manage money, but I did have faith in Brother John Morgan. I believed he knew how to order my steps in order to get me out of debt.

I did everything he told me to do, each and every day, without reservation. And the results were nothing short of miraculous. We got out of debt in about 7 months and have been debt free for over 20 years. Not only that, by doing everything he said to do, my wife was able to quit her job and become a full time homemaker and mother.

Why do I tell you this story? There are some of you who are at the same place I was, and you do not know what to do next.   Nothing has worked. Depression has taken over and you are unable to function at even the most rudimentary level. You have no emotional energy left and hope is only a memory. If this is you, the following list is for you.

This is a list of things to do each and every day. Just as I had faith in my pastor's expertise, you must have faith in **my** expertise when I tell you that if you follow these daily steps, each and every day, you will once again gain purpose and hope and you WILL get a job and get a job quickly.

On the following page, you will find a Checklist (Figure 6) to use everyday. Make copies of this, mark off each items you do it in order. Do not stop until all items are checked off. Use it everyday until it becomes routine.

The Daily Steps to Get a Job Checklist

Date ___ / ___ / ___

[ ] **Start your morning at 6:00 AM with a 20 minute walk.** If you are physically unable to walk for 20 minutes start at 5 minutes and work up.

[ ] **When you finish your walk, shower and dress for work.** If you are a blue-collar worker, this means clean work clothes. If you are a white-collar worker, clean shirt and tie or a business dress if you are a woman.

[ ] **Eat something with a small amount of fat content** The brain must have fat to operate properly.

[ ] **Get your list of prospects (Job Communications Log Sheet/*PowerNetworking* form 5A/B) and start calling at 7:30 AM.** Decision makers are often in the office early.

[ ] **Do not stop until you have talked to 24 people.**

[ ] **Call someone other than a family member and give them a debrief on your morning's activities.** Good and bad. What worked and what did not work. How you felt. **This is not an option.** Find a friend to whom you can be accountable. Knowing you will have to give an account to your friend will keep you active.

[ ] **Do NOT** get on the Internet or read the newspaper until you have made your 24 calls.

[ ] **Find some volunteer work one day a week:** hospitals, retirement homes, schools, churches, sports, Boy Scouts.

[ ] **Go to a house of worship at least once a week.** And when you go, 'be there.' Concentrate on what is sung and what is said.

Figure 6

Accountability.   A word about finding someone to report to: **It is extremely important to find someone to whom you will be accountable**. This needs to be someone who will help you keep track of your progress, someone who will support you no matter what you do each day or don't do each day. This needs to be someone other than a family member and someone who will not chastise you, but rather lift you up and encourage you.

You need to make your last call of the day to this person. If you know that you will have to give an account of your calls, you will become motivated to make them. You will somehow have the strength to make the next call knowing that you will be reporting on your progress each day.

Get a job 80% faster. Studies have shown that people who have an accountability partner generally go to work 80% faster than those who do not.

Remember: *The rich get richer because the rich do what the rich do…*

"Knowledge comes by eyes always open and working hard, and there is no knowledge that is not power."
-Jeremy Taylor (1613-1667)
English Bishop

Telephone Scripts

OK, you are well on your way:

- You have your courage stake (No fear!). *Tool#4*
- You have your daily activities (Just DO it!). *Tool#6*
- You have your vertical marketing call lists. *Tool#5*
- You have an effective method to track your calls. *Tool#5*

So what do you say on the phone???

The 'Pros' use scripts. First, understand that professional phone callers ALL use written scripts. So, if you are going to sound like a pro, use the tools the pros use. In this case the tools are written telephone scripts. Why is this so important?

Frees you to listen. The first reason to use a script is that it frees you to concentrate on listening. It will become obvious after making a few calls that every person with whom you speak is different. Each person has everyday trials and stresses like you do. Each has ups and downs. Each has a distinct personality, tone of voice, cadence, etc. Having a script allows you to listen to 'how' each speaks, not just to what he says. This gives you the advantage you need to get the information you want. It is the script that gives you this advantage. You will be able to really 'hear' the other person.

Lowers your stress level.   The second reason for reading from a script is that making up your script 'on the fly' always raises the level of tension in your voice. This is because you do not want to make a mistake. This anxiety is 'heard' on the phone and it will make the listener uncomfortable.

Document objections.   The third reason for having a written script is to allow you to document the objections. Every objection you encounter should be documented. After a while you will notice that there are only about 4 or 5 different objections (we discuss these later). Documenting these objections will enable you to be able to answer each one the next time you receive one. In addition, documenting their objections will enable you to 'fine tune' your script.

Objectives for canvassing friends & family

Phone script objectives.   Before creating a script, understand that each phone-calling script must have an objective. Since you will be calling 2 separate groups (friends/family and companies), you will have 3 distinct objectives:

- Inform each of your contacts that you are unemployed and actively looking for work.
- Ask each to please actively assist you in your search efforts.
- Obtain accurate contact information (email address, phone numbers, cell numbers, etc.)

After you have created the script, print it in large letters and place it where you can read it standing up. Yes, standing up. You sound better on the phone when you are standing. This is a tool the professionals use.

Practice reading your script. After you have written your script (or copied one of these), practice reading the script out loud. If you are serious about your efforts, tape-record your reading of the script. When you play back the recording, you will be surprised at how it sounds. Listen for voice inflections that say you are frightened or nervous. Listen for words that do not sound clear or sound run together. Say each word clearly. Strive for clear declarative sentences with pauses between each sentence.

Practice with a friend. After you have rehearsed your script with a tape recorder, call someone you know and ask if you can practice your scripts with him. Ask his opinion as to how you sound. Did it sound sincere, 'canned', too fast, too slow? Plan on reading the same script at least 10 times before you start canvassing your list.

After rehearsing your script 10 times, you will begin to memorize it. This is good; however, continue to read the script each time you make the calls. Remember, the reason you are reading it is because doing so *frees your mind to concentrate on listening.* As a reminder, all professional phone callers read their scripts.

Sample script for friends and family

Lets look at a sample script. This script is designed to be copied and placed in front of you when you do your calling. It is written in large letters so as to be easily read.

"Practice does NOT make perfect...
    Perfect practice makes perfect."
                              -Ben Hogan (1912-1997)
                              Professional golfer

Phone Script #1
for Family, Friends, Acquaintances

"Hello _____, this is (your first name)
(pause…) (your last name).
Tom, **I NEED YOUR HELP**. (pause…)
I find myself looking for work and am
hoping that you might know of someone
who can make use of my talents?

As you may know, my last position was
with (company)_____
as a (position) _____
Do you know of anyone I might contact?
(contact name) _____
May I use your name when I call him? _____
Also may send you my resume for your
reference?_____
Let me make sure I have your correct
mailing address and email address.
(check your contact information)
(his/her name)_____, thank you for all
your help.   Please let me know of any
possible leads you might think of. I will keep
you informed as to my progress."
Thank you so much.

Now, lets look at this script:

- First, you have contacted Tom and *humbly* ask him for his help.
- Second, you described your situation.
- Third, you have asked if he knows anyone who can use you.
- Fourth, you asked permission to use his name.
- Fifth, you asked if you can send him your resume
- Sixth, you established the correct contact information.
- Finally, you thanked him.

If he is like the majority of people, Tom will do whatever he can to help you.

Why will Tom go out of his way to help you? Because deep down, Tom knows that he could some day be just like you: looking for work. He knows he is one 'pink slip' away from being in the same boat you are. We live in a world of uncertainty and people recognize the need to help others when they can. Tom will help.

To help you understand this, have someone read this script to you as if you were Tom. If you are like most people, you will experience the emotion of compassion. This will automatically cause you to want to help in any way that you can. Why is this?

This conversation does something very subliminal to the listener. This conversation triggers a change in his subconscious mind (that part of his inner self that works below the surface). This subconscious part of our minds is always working on problems.

> For example, have you ever tried to remember the name of a particular movie actor but just could not. You stopped thinking about it and 2 hours later, for no apparent reason, the name just 'popped' into your head.

This is your subconscious at work. Your subconscious mind continues to work on the problem even when your conscious mind quits.

Once you have asked your friend for help, and he attaches an emotional link to your situation, he has created a subconscious tension that will look for resolution. The term for this is subconscious dissidence. This tension will cause a person to subconsciously and continuously look for ways and people to help you, in order to resolve this dissidence in his subconscious.

OK, you have contacted all of your personal contacts. It is now time to effectively begin canvassing companies you want to work for.

"Wherever there is a human being there is an opportunity for a kindness."
                              - Seneca (B.C. 3-65 A.D.)

Scripts for canvassing companies

The objectives of these scripts are:

1. Locate the decision maker.
2. Get an appointment.

3. NOTHING ELSE!!!

Notice the objective is NOT to find out if there are any jobs available, nor to tell them how great you are, nor find out if you can send them your resume. NO. The only thing you want to do in a telephone call is to first, **locate the decision maker** and second **get an appointment**. As you start making phone calls and locating decision makers, you will be sending resumes and discussing your qualifications. *But* your initial objective is ONLY to locate the decision maker and get an appointment.

We will list several sample scripts. Feel free to copy each and place them directly above your desk when you begin calling. Remember to always read your script and do not attempt to "wing it".

Script#2
Company Campaign Script:

(Call to the main switchboard)

Hello, my name is (your first name) (Pause) (your last name). **I NEED YOUR HELP!!**

Who is in charge of your _____ department?

How do you spell his name? _____

Does he have a direct number? _____

Thank you, you have been so helpful!

 What is your name? _____

Thank you, (his name), you are wonderful!

Would you please transfer me?

Mr._____,

My name is (your first name) (pause) (your last name), **I NEED YOUR HELP...**

I understand that you are in charge of the _____department.

I would like to explore how I may possibly help you in your efforts.

*May I come see you tomorrow at 2:00?

OK, lets look at this script. This is the initial call to a company you could possibly work for. You call the main number (from your Job Communications Log Sheet, Figure 5B). The first question is designed to **locate the decision maker.** You ask who is in charge of the department you could possibly work in. You will write down this name and phone number on your Job Communications Log Sheet.

Next, you ask for the receptionist's name. Document this name as well. You may have occasion to pass along a complement about her to a decision maker within the company.

You then ask if she could transfer the call.

(Note: If you get a voice mailbox, you will leave a message designed to get the person to return your call, which we will discuss later in this chapter.)

When the department head answers the phone, you then:
- Ask for his help.
- State that you would like to help him in his efforts. This tells him in a more pleasant manner that you are looking for work.
- Ask for a personal meeting on a specific time and day.

Ask for the appointment on a specific time and day. If you have been paying attention, you will notice a rather direct question in the script: "May I come see you tomorrow at 2:00?" This is a very important sentence. It asks for a personal meeting on a specific day at a specific time. At first, this may seem rather bold. But let me assure you that it is not. In fact, it is rather welcomed by the listener. How can that be???

Responsibilities of typical manager. Let me explain the responsibilities of the typical department manager. Department managers are responsible for directing people in producing a product or service. Their performance is in direct relation to the quality of people working for them. Good managers are ALWAYS on the look out for good people... whether or not they can use them right now. And remember, managers talk to other managers. They are kindred spirits with similar problems when it comes to qualified workers. When you make contact with a manager, your name and resume may likely be distributed around the company. So, the first realization you must have is that managers want to know about good people... like YOU.

Next, good managers are always **controlled by a calendar**. They have meetings to go to, deadlines to meet, vacations to keep track of, reports to generate, etc. All managers keep track of these on their calendars. When you ask for a meeting on a specific day at a specific time, they automatically go to their calendar to see if they are free to meet with you. If they do not have a conflict, the majority of the time they say, "YES!"

If you are skeptical about asking for the meeting don't be. This technique works!

I attempted to prove that 'asking for the meeting on a specific time and date' would not work. I made five cold calls and asked for the appointment. To my shock and amazement, of the five, three gave me the appointment when I asked and the other two gave me the appointment at a different time. *100% success rate at getting the appointment!*

Like Nike says...

"Just Do It!"

Script #3
Consulting Company Script

Hello, my name is <u>(your first name)</u> (pause) <u>(your last name)</u> . **I NEED YOUR HELP!!**
Does your company do IT consulting?
Does your company provide turnkey project services, such as PeopleSoft, SAP, Seibol?
Who is responsible for those projects?_____
What is his title?_____
Thank you, you have been a huge help.
What is your name?_____
Thank you, <u>(his name),</u> would you please transfer me?

Mr. _____, my name is <u>(your first name)</u> (pause) <u>(your last name).</u>
I NEED YOUR HELP.
I have been informed that you are responsible for the _____ project, is this correct?
I have a great deal of experience with such projects and would like to discuss possibly joining your team.
*May I come by tomorrow at 2:00 so we can discuss my qualifications?

Voice Mail:
'The good the bad and the ugly'

Ah, what about voice mail? A fact of life is that 80% of the calls we make are answered by a machine. UGH! So how do you get them to return your call?

When you leave a voice message, say:

Hello, Mr. Smith, my name is
<u>(your first name)</u> (pause...) <u>(your last name)</u> (pause...).
Tom Johnson (someone within the company) instructed me to call you.
I NEED YOUR HELP.
If you would please call me, my number is
713 (pause) **555** (pause) **1234** (pause) **thank you.**

Now, lets look at this message:
- You have given your name clearly by leaving a pause between your first and last names. This allows them to write it down easily.
- You have 'dropped a name' from someone within their company. (You retrieved this name your Job Communications Log Sheet. It may only be the receptionist.)
- You have asked for help.
- Last, you have clearly given a phone number.

If he is like most business people, he will make a call to one of 2 people: either to the name you dropped (to ask about you) or to you directly. Most often they will take the path of least resistance and simply call you back.

Final word on telephone scripts. Telephone scripts are designed to get you to the decision maker and get you an appointment. The phone scripts presented to you *will work.* However, realize that you can only control what YOU say on the phone. The other person will always ask questions and/or raise objections. This is OK. When it happens, simply respond as necessary but focus on a 'face-to-face' meeting. This dialog is normal and is part of the telephone process. After you have made a number of calls, you will begin to see a pattern to the listener's questions. After a short while, you will have heard all the responses and questions.

In wrapping up our discussion on the use of telephone scripts, keep in mind these key points:

- Professional telephone callers ALL use scripts.
- Your objective of the call is to locate the decision maker, get an appointment, NOTHING ELSE.
- Reading your script frees you to concentrate on listening.
- Ask for an appointment on a specific date and time.

"True bravery is shown by performing without witness what one might be capable of doing before all the world."
                        -La Rochefoucauld (1613-1680)
                              French classical writer

Common Responses to Calls

In your telephone campaign, you will receive some common responses. These responses are to be expected and prepared for. Over the years, we have observed managers most often respond to cold calls from potential employees with one or more questions.

You may hear these exact questions or some variations. Being prepared with a response is very important. How you answer these questions will largely determine whether or not you get the appointment. You would do well to rehearse these with a friend over the phone. The time to address each question is *before* they are asked.

Question #1:
"What are your qualifications?"
Your response:
"(You give your 30 second bio (see Appendix B))
+ I would greatly like to expand on this. May I please come by tomorrow at 2:00?"

Note: A '30 second bio' is what you would tell a total stranger about yourself if you met one in an elevator. It is your advertisement. You have 30 seconds to tell him your skills and qualifications. (See Appendix B for instructions on how to create a personal bio along with various examples.)

Question #2,

"Send me your resume."

Your response:

 "I will certainly do that, but I believe we would both be better served if I hand delivered it in order to 'breathe life' into my resume. May I drop it by tomorrow at 2:00?"

Question #3:

"All our hiring goes through HR."

Your Response:

"I certainly understand and respect that; however, I hope you can understand my desire to distinguish my resume among the 1000's they receive. May I please come by tomorrow at 2:00?"

Question #4:

"We are not hiring, in fact we are laying off."

Your response:

"I am sorry to hear that. I do hope your job is secure. I would still like to come meet you. I would like to become part of your network in the event you get laid off, as well. May I come by tomorrow at 2:00?"

Final thoughts to ponder

Good managers want to know you. It is important to remember that *good* managers are always looking for good people. Even if they cannot use you at the moment, they know that having good people at their disposal is vital to their performance. These managers will welcome an opportunity to meet a person who can possibly be an asset to them. Your calling and wanting to meet with them is helping them in their jobs.

It is also important to remember that as a professional in your field, you will be speaking with other professionals in the same field. This common ground gives both of you a purpose for meeting each other. Even if the person has no opportunity to help you, *you*, on the other hand, may have an opportunity to help *him*. After all, you are actively looking in the job market and may possibly pass along a lead to the manager you have met. Professionals are wise to network with other professionals.

You have options at your disposal. Being a displaced worker gives you options that are unlimited. You have an unlimited number of companies you can contact. You have total freedom to call 1000 companies a month, if you choose to. This option means that if one company chooses not to speak to you, you can bury them in the trash by simply **making the next phone call**. After all, if they were not open to knowing about qualified people, you would not want to work for them anyway. Don't fret about it; just make the next call.

> A major insurance company gives each of its professional phone callers $5 for each "no" they receive on the telephone. They know that after 35 "no"s, they will get a $1,000 sale.

Your telephone calling is putting money in the bank. Each time you make a phone call, you are putting money in your pocket because each call does 2 things:

First, it most likely put your resume into the hands of a decision maker, a person who is in your industry and could possibly use you, or may know someone who could use you.

Second, you have met a decision maker and have developed some type of rapport, which could eventually be turned into a networking contact. This could definitely put money into your account, as we will discuss in the next section entitled *"Power Networking"*

"The sense of this word among the Greeks affords the noblest definition of it: *'Enthusiasm'* signifies *God in us*."
-Germaine De Stael (1766-1817)

"Every great and commanding moment in the annals of the world is the triumph of some *enthusiasm*."
- Emerson (1803-1882)

Interview Techniques Overview

The first 8 Tools in your toolbox gave you the tools necessary to **locate decision makers** and **get the appointment**. This was accomplished by your understanding of the power of the telephone as well as a systematic method of tracking your phone activity.

People skills. This next section deals with what to do once you get face to face with the decision maker. You will learn:

- How to distinguish yourself in the interview process
- How to read body language
- How to communicate at a level that makes the other person 'like' you

In short, you will be given the 'people skills' you need to propel your job search as well as your career.

A most irksome question: *"How many times have you seen someone get the job who was less qualified, had less experience and was generally inferior in their ability to do the job?"*

If you have been in business for any length of time, you will say, "I have seen this many times." Over and over again, we have witnessed less qualified people being promoted; the prize given to the one who least deserves it. History has shown us that it is not always the most educated, the most experienced, or the most qualified person who gets the job. It is not the smartest person in the office that gets the promotion. It is not the problem solver that gets ahead. It is not the person who 'deserves' the position. If this is the case, the question is:

"Why do *they* get the job and *you* don't?"

To effectively answer this question, we must explore some basic elements of human nature.

Human nature. The first element we need to uncover and understand is just how people make decisions.

How people make decisions

Most of the decisions we, as adults, make in our life are based on *emotions*. We then rationalize our decisions with *facts*.

Madison Avenue learned this long ago. They have known that people purchase automobiles based not on facts, but on emotions. For example, in their ads, they portray a young, successful professional driving a Lexus down Wall Street Avenue in Manhattan. The obvious emotional link is that "if *you* drive a Lexus, you *too* will be successful like this Wall Street stockbroker."

Think about this for a moment. The primary function of an automobile is to transport you from point A to point B. It is *not* to make you a successful stockbroker!

Another example is the hard-hat, tool-belt wearing steel worker jumping into his white Ford F150 on the job site of a major construction project. If you work construction, you identify with the hard-hat and have an emotional link to the driver and his truck. After all, if it is good enough for him, it is good enough for you.

We make decisions based on emotions and back up our decisions with facts.

If you think about this, you know this to be the case. For example, if you are married, did you choose your mate on the basis of statistics (facts) or did you make your decision with your emotions? Or when you bought that new dress, you emotionally *wanted* the dress and after buying it, told yourself all the good reasons for doing so, like: "The color goes perfectly with my shoes", or "I needed a dress that wasn't too *dressy*." Or even better, "My new shotgun *is* the best in its category according to Shooting Magazine." (Nevermind about the other 4 shotguns you already have and don't use!!)

These are all emotional decisions supported by facts. The point to be made here is this:

People are also <u>hired</u> based on emotions.

This is the way it has always been and this is the way it will always be; it is not ever going to change. If this is the case, and it is, how do you use this fact to your advantage?

Create a positive emotional response. If you know people decide whom they will hire based on emotions, you must relate to people so as to *create a positive emotional response.*

This section on "Interviewing Techniques," Tools #9 - #14, is designed to give you the tools necessary to create that positive emotional response in other people, specifically the people with whom you interview. This positive emotional response will distinguish *you* among your competition. It is designed to make you 'stand out' in their mind as *the* person who is clearly the best candidate for the position. It is designed to make you *emotionally* desirable. It is designed to make them 'feel' good about you.

If you put into practice what is presented in this section, you will get more job offers, influence more people, and be in control of relationships to the benefit of both parties. Your influence will grow and people will see you as a leader in your field. You will get the promotions and you will rise to the top wherever you are, professionally or personally.

If this all sounds like a 'snake oil magic elixir' to some, I invite you to prove me wrong. I have had many testimonials from people who have practiced what you will learn. Here is an example of a typical testimonial that I have received:

...Using your interview techniques, I asked _____ for help in finding instructor opportunities. She agreed to meet with me after I completed my exam. Well, we had an excellent 2-hour conversation about continuing education and distance education, during which I used *your pacing techniques*. At the end of our conversation, she asked for my resume and gave me the names and telephone numbers of 4 contacts that directly manage the continuing education/corporate programs within the HCC system. The best part is that she said the magic words, ***"I have a good feeling about you!"*** This could not have happened without *your help*. *Your suggestions really work.* I am pursuing the other contacts and will be applying all the techniques that you taught the group. And I look forward to using them as I widen my job campaign.

Kind Regards, **A. Matutis**

The 4 P's of Interviewing

The actual interview process is divided into four sections:

- **P**reparation
- **P**resentation
- **P**acing
- **P**ersistence

We call them the four P's of Interviewing. The Presentation tool is augmented with a tool entitled "Topic of Money."

Topic of money.   The topic of money will always come up. Knowing how to address the issue will make you a winner, not a loser. This tool will definitely assure you of the best possible compensation package to be had once you are offered the position.

So sit back, open your mind; make the *quality decision* to learn what others have learned. You are well on your way. And oh, by the way, it will be fun...

"To be fond of learning is near to wisdom."
-Confucius (B.C. 551-479)

Preparation

This is the first step in the interview process, the first "P." If you have been invited to an interview, it can be assumed that you have passed their requirements for adequate education, credentials and/or experience. You may also have passed their requirements of being a 'kindred' spirit (one who is in the same profession or discipline). Remember that an audience with the decision maker, *not the HR department*, is what you want. The goal is to distinguish yourself in the interview. In order to 'stand out' in the interviewer's mind, you must act like a good Boy Scout; you must 'Be Prepared.'

The interview process begins long before you get in front of the decision maker. You must prepare yourself ahead of time for the interview. In order to do this, there are several things you must do.

"S.O.A.R." like an eagle. The first step in your preparation is to devote to writing your past accomplishments. These will be success stories in your line of work. These are the 'home runs' you hit while you were employed. These stories illustrate just how

valuable you are. They are proof that you can do the job and do it better than anyone else.

To help you in this, we will use a simple form called "S.O.A.R." * (Form 10A).

*Note: "S.O.A.R." is used by permission of Lee Hecht Harrison, Global Career Management Services, a leader in the outplacement services business. For additional information, log onto www.LHH.com.

"S.O.A.R." stands for:

Situation
        Opportunity
                Action
                        Results

"S.O.A.R."

Situation: _____

_____

_____

Opportunity: _____

_____

_____

Action: _____

_____

_____

_____

Results: _____

_____

_____

(Figure 10A)

Here is how "S.O.A.R." works...

Situation: "When I was a production supervisor, I observed that we routinely wasted 4% of the stamped parts because of a quality control failure."

Opportunity: "I was given permission to evaluate the rejected parts for the purpose of improving the process."

Action: "I contacted the engineering department and asked for an in-depth analysis of the rejects. They noticed that the raw materials were not of consistent quality. This caused some parts to be rejected during the manufacturing process."

Result: "The vendor was required to deliver a different material which resulted in a drop in rejects from 4% to less than ½%. This totaled an additional $175,000 revenue per year to the company."

Now, lets look at this "S.O.A.R." In these 7 sentences, I have relayed a story that shows my ability to:
- Accurately observe situations.
- Willingly go above and beyond to solve problems.
- Rally the resources to find the solution.
- And add to the bottom line of the company.

And I told you all this within about 20 seconds.

A "S.O.A.R." is a story...a success story...a story with which the other person can identify...a story that shows that you understand *his* business and that you are able to solve *his* problems. Also, understand that people are hired to solve problems. Your "S.O.A.R.s" will establish you as a problem solver.

Common problems. In all businesses, there are common problems within each industry. If you have been working in a specific industry, you know of these problems. You have 'lived' them. As you are interviewing, you will be presented with opportunities to tell your "S.O.A.R.s" to the interviewer. These "S.O.A.R.s" (situation, opportunity, action, results) will show the person your ability to solve problems. Most likely, these are the *same problems he is facing*. This will distinguish you among all of the other people interviewing for the same position. This is to say that when you leave, the interviewer will 'feel' good about your ability to solve 'his' problems.

Lets look at another "S.O.A.R.":

   Situation: "I was building custom cabinets in custom built homes using birch solid core plywood. I believed we were wasting too much material because of damage to the wood by the forklift used in transporting it from the warehouse to the job site."

   Opportunity: "I spoke with the foreman about contacting the manufacturer directly concerning the problem and he said, 'OK.' "

   Action: "I called the manufacturer and told him the problem and he suggested having the material directly shipped to the jobsite in the containers designed to assure no shipment damage."

Results: "The foreman agreed to have the materials directly shipped to the jobsite and we stopped waste by almost 20%. It also reduced the cost of materials by 6% due to the direct shipment."

Here's another "S.O.A.R.":

Situation: "The division warehouse sent defective parts back to the manufacturer for repair. Over time, we saw that we had over $1 million in inventory out for repair."

Opportunity: "I decided to closely track the turnaround time for each manufacturer for repair of parts. I found that the manufacturers were not returning our parts in a timely fashion. Some were keeping our parts for many months or not returning them at all."

Action: "I designed a tracking system for these parts using bar coding software. I generated aging reports on each part and had a clerk contact the manufacturers daily to check on the status of the individual parts that had not been returned in the allotted time."

Results: "This process lowered the parts out for repair from one million dollars to approximately $180,000. In addition, because of the increased inventory, we were able to lower our standing inventory by almost $500,000."

Another "S.O.A.R.":

Situation: "Our division was responsible for all voice and data communications for the company. We provided the services and billed the business units proportionally for what they used. When I joined the team, we were $12 million under recovered."

Opportunity: "I was given the directive to 'get the $12 million.' "

Action: "I utilized a staff of accountants and programmers and quickly discovered that the old tracking system had no 'checks and balances' built in. It was a rudimentary database woefully inadequate for the task. We designed an Access database and transferred the data from the old database. We instituted the logical checks and balances."

Results: "We were able to bill the $12 million within about 8 months and actually finished the year $500,000 in the black. As a side benefit, our program allowed each call center manager to check his bill on line in real time. Because the program was PC based, we lowered our mainframe cost by about $50,000 per year."

One last "S.O.A.R.":

Situation: "I was responsible for all the travel arrangements for 4 executives who traveled a great deal. "

Opportunity: "I looked closely at each person's travel history and noticed several things that I could do that might make life a little easier for them.'"

Action: "I met with each executive and showed him that if I made several routing changes I could cut about 4 - 10 days travel time per year for each executive. They gave me permission to make the changes. I also introduced them to train travel, which they loved."

Results: "The following year we cut travel time by almost 30 days total for all 4 executives and, I am glad to say, created happier bosses."

Devote your "S.O.A.Rs" to writing. I cannot over emphasize the importance of this exercise. Let me explain. Devoting your "S.O.A.R.s" to writing does three things. First, it will cause you to realize just how *valuable you are.* These "S.O.A.R.s" will cause you to say to yourself,   "Hey...I really am good at what I do!!!" Second, writing your "S.O.A.R.s" will allow you to build confidence in yourself and what you can do. Third, writing down your "S.O.A.R.s" helps you practice telling your story so that you can relay it during the interview quickly and accurately.

How to use your "S.O.A.R.s"

At some point in your interview, you will find an opportunity to tell one or more of your "S.O.A.R.s". It will usually be when the two of you are 'talking shop'. At this point, you will notice a situation or condition within his business that matches one of your "S.O.A.R.s". Don't forget, all similar businesses have similar problems.

Memorize at least three "S.O.A.R.s." To be effective using your "S.O.A.R.s," *you must memorize at least three.* Memorize them well so that you can easily give them within 20 - 30 seconds. They must be delivered smoothly and effortlessly. You cannot struggle to remember details. No, memorizing three of your "S.O.A.R."s will free you to concentrate on how the listener is receiving your story.

Short declarative sentences. When you write your "S.O.A.R.s", make short declarative sentences of 17 words or less; the shorter, the better. Use as many facts as are necessary to give your "S.O.A.R.s" *weight.* For example, "I saved the company $200,000" sounds much better than "I saved the company a lot of money." Also, using percentages is good, but it is even better when you attach dollar amounts to them, such as, " I reduced rejects by 18% which totaled $12,555.00 per year."

A very important note concerning "S.O.A.R.s" if you are struggling in your job search.

If you are depressed about your *perceived* inability to get a job, writing your "S.O.A.R.s" can help your emotional well-being. Devoting to writing your past accomplishments will help give you the self-confidence that you need to get a job. If you cannot seem to find any job-related "S.O.A.R.s", find non-job related "S.O.A.R.s". Everyone has some: so think back to a time when you "S.O.A.R.ed." It could be when you were a child, or a student. Find some story that can be documented as a "S.O.A.R." and write it down. You have the time, so you have no excuse. The effort of writing down your stories will prompt you to remember more and more. You just have to start the process.

Depression

Depression is a very real condition that people face. Being unemployed can fan the flames of depression for any number of reasons. There are physical reasons for depression as well as emotional reasons. If you are suffering from lingering depression, get help. Help is to be had from any number of sources. Reaching out is the first step in getting relief.

"Do not brood over your past mistakes and failures as this will only fill your mind with grief, regret and depression. Do not repeat them in the future."

-Sivananda (born 1887)
Indian physician

Fifteen years ago, I became hopelessly depressed after being laid off from a company I planned to retire from. I was scared, and ultimately depressed because I could not find a job. I began telling myself that I could not do anything. What was even worse, I started believing it. When I was deeply depressed, I hired a coach that told me to do what I am instructing you to do. He told me to devote my "S.O.A.R.s" to writing. So I started writing my "S.O.A.R.s". I started writing "S.O.A.R.s" about everything I ever did in life...not just business related. I started my "S.O.A.R.s" when I was in the 5th grade. This was when I joined the school band and became the best clarinet player in the band. I made this one of my "S.O.A.R.s". I later became an Eagle Scout and made this one of my "S.O.A.R.s". I included events throughout my life, personal and business. I spent 28 hours handwriting my "S.O.A.R.s" and completed over 40 of them. (I wasn't working, so I certainly had the time to devote to it.) And much to my surprise, it was a turning point in my life. After writing my "S.O.A.R.s," I realized that I DID have skills that were valuable and that I WAS good at what I did and that ANY company would be fortunate to have me on their team. The transformation from an "I can't do anything" attitude to an "I CAN do anything" was nothing short of miraculous.

The previous story is designed to help you if you are depressed and discouraged. If you are in this category, completing your "S.O.A.R.s" is critical for you. This cannot be over emphasized. **You MUST devote these to writing.** Why is this so important?

It has been said that 'our thoughts become clear through the writings of our pens'. The discipline of devoting these "S.O.A.R.s" to writing will organize your thoughts about the successes in your life. Writing your "S.O.A.R.s" will greatly increase your self-esteem. It also has another tremendous benefit. It enables you to 'look smart' in front of the interviewer.

"The great art of writing is the art of making people real to themselves with words."
-Logan Smith (1865-1946)
American author

Folks who ramble. If you are a person who tends to 'ramble' when you talk, try to construct simple sentences with pauses between each sentence. This is important.   The easier you are to understand, *the smarter you are perceived to be.* A good pattern to follow is the speeches of the President of The United States. His speeches are designed to be clearly understood by most anybody. If you look closely at his speeches, you will find they following 3 simple guidelines:

- Simple declarative sentences.
- Pauses between each sentence.
- Longer pause between each major thought.

Use this formula when you construct and practice your "S.O.A.R.s." It will also serve you well in your personal conversations. To strike your thinking, read the following "S.O.A.R.s" and decide which one sounds better...number 1 or 2:

#1. "I worked in construction for a company that never seemed to keep track of their payroll. They were always correcting something on my check. We were contracted to build a school in Pasadena that was the most awful color red you can imagine. My job was to keep track of the deliveries onsite for the general contractor. I did the best I could, considering there was no air conditioning in the foreman's shed. I was able to keep ahead of schedule by talking with the foundation crew chief so as to have the rebar and forms delivered before they arrived on site. What I did enabled the foundation to be poured before the rains started."

Or...

#2. "I worked for a general contractor who was building a school in Pasadena. I was responsible for keeping track of deliveries to the job site. I made sure that the rebar and forms were delivered *before* the foundation crew arrived. This meant that the foundation was completed before the weather turned bad."

I believe you get the point. **Simple is better.**

"I always turn to the sports pages first, which records people's accomplishments. The front page has nothing but man's failures."
                              -Earl Warren (1891-1974)

The next step in **Preparation** is what is called:

Detective work

This includes finding out as much about the company as you can. This information is available in a number of locations.   A good start is the Internet.   Most companies have web sites that have information you need to know BEFORE you set foot on the premises. Another source of information is the public library. Ask the librarian for help in researching the company or companies with whom you will be interviewing. She will lead you to the research section that contains the current information on most companies.

Another source of company information is the company's salesmen. Most salesmen will be happy to meet with you to give you insights into their company. When you speak with them, ask them questions about the company's culture.   How do they treat their employees? How do they treat their customers? What is their perception of the 'man at the top' of the company?   When you research the company, make note of the names of the officers and managers. Dropping a name always makes you look good.   Again remember that this effort is to make you look smart when you are in the interview.

As you do your research, it is important to document this information for reference. An excellent tool for this is the Job Campaign Communications Log Sheet (Figure 5B and Tool #5 for detailed explanation).

Topic of Money. The topic of money is covered in detail in Tool#13, but we will introduce the topic here.

What does it take for you to live? The final item to prepare for is the topic of money. First, you must determine how much is required for you to live. Not how much you think you are worth, but rather what it costs to maintain your standard of living. If you do not know this amount, get your last several years' tax returns from when you were working. Total these and divide by the number of months.

For example: if you earned $48,000 in 2002 and $49,500 in 2003. This totals a gross amount of $97,500 for the 24 months. Divide this number by 24 to get an average amount per month. This equals $4062.50 per month or $44,750.00 per year.

You need to know this number before you begin any discussion of money. Why? Because this will be the least you can accept for the position. Accepting anything less will automatically add to your stress level. Now that you know this number, DO NOT share it with anyone, *especially in the interview.*

Next, do your homework in determining what your skill set and experience should command in the workforce. You can do this by going to the Internet. The Internet has a host of websites dedicated to showing you average salaries for various types of work. A simple search on a web site such as google.com on "average salary for carpenter" will return a host of sites that have this information. Know this before you go to the interview.

Ok, you have:
- Devoted your "S.O.A.R.s" to writing.
- Memorized the top 3 "S.O.A.R.s" so that they are easily given in the interview.

- Done your detective work in investigating the companies you will be contacting.
- Determined what your minimum income requirements are.

"A well-prepared mind hopes in adversity."
- Horace (B.C. 65-8)

"There is no road too long to the man who advances deliberately and without undue haste; there are no honors too distant to the man who prepares himself for them with patience."
-La Bruyere (1645-1696)

You are now ready to "present" yourself to the decision maker. This is the second "**P**" in the interview process and is addressed in the next Tool.

Presentation

The second "P" in the interview process is **Presentation**.

Green eggs and ham. As children we grew up with Dr. Seuss and his green eggs and ham. Do you remember the children's story of *Green Eggs and Ham*? In this story, the main character attempts to get Sam to eat the green eggs and ham. Sam always replies, 'I do not like green eggs...'

And neither do you...

Why? Because good eggs are *not* green. Good eggs are white with a yellow yoke. The book takes 25 pages before Sam is convinced to eat the green eggs. If the eggs had been white, Sam would have eaten them on the first page...

How food looks, matters. As any chef will tell you, a person *first* eats with his eyes. If the food presentation does not look enticing, the person will *automatically* be prepared to dislike the way it tastes.

Why tell this story? **Because how you look is crucial to the interview process.** This cannot be over emphasized.   People make value judgments about others solely based on the way they look.

To prove this point, you are going to look at several photos.   After seeing each, you will be asked several questions.

What is her profession?

Can you trust her?

Would she hurt you?

Does she have your best interests at heart?

What is his profession?

Can he be trusted to do the right thing?

Would you call him if you were in trouble?

Does he have your best interests at heart?

What is her profession?

Can you trust her?

Would she be a threat to you?

Does your heart go out to her?

What is his profession?

Would you trust him?

Could he hurt you?

Would you be on your guard around him?

Value judgments. The point to this exercise is that we *immediately* make value judgments on people solely based on how they look. And we make these value judgments within seconds of seeing them. This bring us to a basic point of human nature:

How we look largely determines how we are received.

It is important to note that your qualifications, experience and education may get you in the door, but if you are 'green eggs and ham' to the interviewer, someone else will get the job. So this begs the question:
"How do you use what you wear to your advantage? "

First, understand that in the world in which we live, there are <u>uniforms</u>. These uniforms tell people a host of things. For instance, a person in shorts, t-shirt, flip flops and sunglasses says, 'I am enjoying my time off.' This same person may later wear a policeman's uniform that says, 'I am an officer of the law and have the power of government backing me in my duties.' Same person, making two very different statements by simply wearing different clothes. The uniform we wear says what we 'do' in our profession.

"Beauty may be but skin-deep; however, it may be herein chronicled that all men desire exactly that shallow attribute in women."
                    -Minna Antrim (fl. 1900)
                    Naked Truths and Veiled Illusions

Wear the uniform. When it comes to the uniform you wear:

- First, do not look like 'green eggs and ham'.
- Second, look like what they *want to see*.

How do you do this? First and foremost, wear the absolute best you have. If you are male, wear a suit that has been cleaned. Yes, a suit, even if you are interviewing for a blue-collar job. If you do not have a suit, wear the best you have that has been washed, and ironed. They will notice your effort to look your absolute best.

If you are female, you have a somewhat greater challenge. First, in the interview process, **do not flaunt your sexuality** by what you wear. *Doing so only makes your competition look more professional.* Again, wear your best. A business suit is always correct. Slacks are acceptable, but short skirts are not. Wear hose. Do not wear shoes that expose the toes. No sleeveless dresses or open blouses. If you have long hair, wear it up. Wear jewelry and makeup sparingly, and little or no perfume. Remember: do not flaunt your sexuality.

Personal hygiene. Body odor is very offensive. Bathe and use deodorant before the interview. Be aware that certain foods will cause an odor. For instance, consumption of garlic will cause the body to emit an odor for 24 hours. Do not eat garlic or onion flavored foods before the interview. Alcohol consumption will produce an odor on your breath as well as through your skin, especially when you perspire during the stress of the interview. If you are a smoker, refrain from smoking when you have on your coat. Also remember that perfumes will not cover up odors, they only add to them. If your body or clothes have an odor, you carry them with you to the interview. It is a good idea to ask someone to evaluate you before you go. Ask them to point out anything that might be offensive.

Hair for men means getting a fresh haircut. It really does make a favorable statement. If you have a beard or mustache, you might consider shaving it off. Psychologists tell us that people with facial hair are not immediately trusted. You can always grow it back when you get the job.

More Details About the Business Uniform

The uniform of business. The uniform for the business world is very specific. For men, you cannot go wrong by wearing a suit and tie, a conservative two or three button suit, preferably 100% wool. If you have had your suit for any length of time, consider taking it to a tailor for an alteration so that it will fit you correctly. Have the suit cleaned. If possible, keep your coat on a hanger until just before the interview.

Your tie makes a powerful statement. Your tie should be what is called a 'power' tie. A power tie is a red/maroon tie with a small consistent design. The front of the tie should just touch the top of your belt.

Red Power Tie, 100% silk

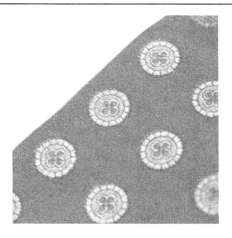

Close-up of Power Tie.

Your shirt matters. Your shirt should be a white, long-sleeved dress shirt with or without button down collar. Do not wear a short-sleeved shirt to an interview. If possible, allow from ¼ to ½ inch of your white shirtsleeve to show at your wrist beneath your coat sleeve. Shirt should be ironed.

Leathers should match. Belt and shoes should be leather and both need to be polished. The color of the leathers should match: either both brown or both black. If you have a leather watchband, it should also match.

Socks/hose. Socks should be black or blue or brown depending on the color of the suit and shoes. If you have trouble keeping your socks up on your calf, get some sock bands. Sagging socks look like 'green eggs and ham.'

Ladies, always wear hose with a dress. They should be neutral in color and fit well. Sagging hose also look like 'green eggs and ham.' Carry an extra pair in case the ones you are wearing get a run just before the interview. Wear low pumps, not sandals, stilettos, or loafers.

Pants. Pants should fit properly, be unwrinkled, and the proper length, just touching the heel of your shoe in the back when you are standing. If you have trouble keeping your pants at your waist, wear suspenders.

Skirt Length. Your skirt, ladies, must come to the middle of your knee or longer. If your skirt exposes your thighs when you are sitting, choose a longer skirt.

Writing instruments make a statement. If you keep writing pens in your shirt pocket, make sure they are not the cheap ballpoint pens. A gold Cross or Mont Blanc pen is the writing instrument of choice. Do not put both pen and pencil in your pocket. If you wear Polo dress shirts that do not have a chest pocket, place it in your inside coat pocket.

Jewelry. All jewelry on men and women makes a statement. If you are married, wear your wedding ring. If you have a ring from your school, fraternity, military, or other organization, wear it. If you wear earrings, men, take them off. Ladies, your earrings should be small. No bracelets. Your watch should be a dress watch, not a plastic sports watch. If you do not have a dress watch, do not wear a watch. All the metal should match. If you have gold rings, your pen, watch and belt buckle should also be gold.

Clean your car. Yes, your car. Managers have been known to escort you to your car. They want to see how you treat your car knowing this is an indication of how you will treat the company's equipment.

Choice of colors. Suit and dress colors vary with the positions for which you apply. **Black** is the most powerful and should be used when applying for upper level management at the president and vice president levels. **Navy blue** is a good choice for customer contact positions such as salesmen and customer service representatives. **Brown** is a good color for mid level positions and is perceived as warm and friendly. Solid colors with very tiny stripes are best. Shy away from bold stripes or patterns. These colors hold true for both men and women. Ladies, no floral designs or bright colors should be worn on any interview.

Women's accessories. Accessories for women such as scarves, hats, purses, etc., are to be used sparingly, and then only in good taste. A good rule of thumb is this: *if it draws attention to itself, DON'T wear it.*

"Women's clothes are painting and men's clothes are sculpture."
                              -Barnett Newman (1905-1970)

Casual vs. suit and tie. You may be going to an interview and the person tells you that they are a casual dress company. What do you wear? *You wear* *the absolute best you have.* This means the wool suit and power tie. They may comment on your suit as being 'overdressed', but they will appreciate your efforts to look your best. You can always dress-down to match the office environment. In addition, your wearing a suit makes your competition look less professional.

OK, you now know how to dress and present yourself in the interview. Remember that if you have done this properly, you have just passed perhaps the most important part of the interview process: the First Impression.

"You never get a second chance to make a first impression."

Truer words have never been spoken.

You have *total* control over how you look. This is a very important part of the interview process and you and *you alone* control how you look. Your efforts for this part of the interview process are very important. Time and money spent in this area will reap great rewards.

Here is a checklist to be used to check your physical appearance before each interview. Copy this list and use it before each interview. Doing so will give you confidence in how you look and will assure you of making a good first impression.

First Impression Check List

Personal Hygiene
[ ] Bathe; use deodorant
[ ] Shave; aftershave
[ ] Brush teeth
[ ] Use mouthwash
[ ] Haircut current
[ ] No body odor
[ ] No breath odor
[ ] Little/no cologne

Dress - ALL
[ ] Suit cleaned/
    wrinkle-free
[ ] Pants proper length
[ ] Shoes polished
[ ] Belt polished
[ ] Socks correct color
[ ] Socks stay up
[ ] Leathers match

Dress - Women
[ ] Hose, neutral color
[ ] Shoes, low pumps
[ ] Dress, correct length
[ ] Do not flaunt
    sexuality
[ ] Purse, small neutral

Dress – Men
[ ] Power tie
[ ] Tie just touching belt
[ ] Pants stay up

Accessories
[ ] Dress watch
[ ] Metals match
[ ] Nice pen
[ ] No hat

Jewelry
[ ] Men, no earrings
[ ] Ladies, small
    earrings
[ ] No bracelets
[ ] Tasteful, does not
    draw attention

Car
[ ] Clean

"Nothing is so contagious as enthusiasm; it moves stones, it charms brutes. Enthusiasm is the genius of sincerity and truth accomplishes no victories without it.

-Bulwer-Lytton (1803-1873)
English poet

Pacing

OK, you have done your **Preparation** for the interview and you now know how to dress for the **Presentation** of yourself visually. We are now going to talk about the actual interview itself with our third "P", **Pacing**.

When you get in front of the decision maker, you have already made a host of impressions with your dress and your handshake (which should be firm and last about 2 seconds). If you have done this properly, you have passed their test of professionalism. It is now time to **'become a member of their tribe'**.

Becoming a member of their tribe.

What do I mean, 'become a member of their tribe?' All companies have a 'tribe' mentality. This is to say that they have a group personality that is made up of the individual tribe members. They have a single purpose, a leader, and ways of interacting with the other tribe members. In order for you to get the job, you MUST be accepted as a member of their tribe.

To reinforce this fact of business life, studies have shown that **97% of the people hired to do a job are** *not totally* **qualified to do the job; BUT 100% of the people hired are** *accepted as a member of the tribe.* You are accepted as one of their own with whom they can work. Managers hire people who can 'fit' into the tribe. Or stated another way, are 'tribal members'.

So how do you become a member of the tribe? To become a member of the tribe, first recognize that it is human nature for us to like people just like us. We gravitate toward people like us and shun people not like us. So, stated simply, you want to *become like* the person with whom you are interviewing so that he will like you. How do you do this?

This technique is called **P**acing. It is a compilation of using your body, voice, and eye movements so as to make the other person comfortable with you by 'acting' just like he does.

You may say, "I don't need to do this; if they don't accept me for who I am, I am certainly not going to change for some silly job!" That is certainly your option. But understand the winners in the job market and life are those who can make other people comfortable around them. This is vital in the interview process. It is the people who can 'Win Friends and Influence People' that get offered the job. **P**acing is the best way to accomplish this.

How Pacing works: Whenever you are in the presence of another person in a one-on-one conversation, force yourself to observe several things:

- Where are his hands?
  - o Are they hidden in his crossed arms?
  - o Are they in his pockets?
  - o Is one hand in one pocket?

Pacing says wherever their hands are; *you casually put yours in the same position.*

- Does he use his hands when expressing himself?
  - o Does he express himself with his palms up or down?
  - o Does he use an index finger to point?
  - o Does he touch his face when speaking?

Pacing says to use your hands in expressing yourself in *the same way he does.*

- How is he sitting in the chair?
  - o Is he leaning back in the chair?
  - o Is he sitting forward in the chair?
  - o Is he slouching in the chair?

Pacing says sit using the *same posture he uses.*

- Listen to how he speaks.
  - o Does he speak slowly?
  - o Does he speak quickly?
  - o Does he pause before answering a question?
  - o Does he begin answering your question before you are finished asking it?

Pacing says to take on the *same rhythm of speaking the other person uses.*

- Watch his eye movements.
  - o Does he 'lock' into your eyes when he talks?
  - o Does he look into space while speaking, but only look into your eyes when making a point or asking a question?
  - o Does he blink a lot when speaking?
  - o Does he not blink at all when speaking?

Pacing says to use his *same eye movements and expressions when you are speaking.*

Why is all this Pacing so important?

When you pace the other person, you will *automatically* put the other person at ease. Why? Because *people feel comfortable with people just like themselves.*

The amazing part of this process is that people do not know you are pacing them; they only know that they 'feel' comfortable around you. And this is what you want. You want them to 'feel' good about you. **P**acing is what makes this happen.

Now that you know *how* to pace a person, it is essential that you practice on everyone with whom you come in contact. Every time you speak with someone, make it a point to pace him. If you diligently (with constant effort) do as I have instructed, you will be shocked at the response you will get from everyone you meet, adults as well as children. This works... so do it to the point that it becomes habitual with everyone you meet.

Hot Buttons. It is very important to realize that people display their 'egos' on their walls, both at home and in their workplace. People display what is important in their lives on their walls in plain view. So, as quickly as you can, scan the walls, shelves, and desktop. Look for pictures of family, diplomas, trophies, awards, and anything else that was put there as a point of pride. Use this information, at some point, to ask a question about their point of pride. Consider this their <u>hot button</u>. If you ask them about it, watch the first reaction on their faces; most often it will be a smile as they look at the object. Pursue the topic by finding some way to complement them on their accomplishment.

Complements. When it comes to complements, you need to know that there are 2 types of complements:
- Un-informed complement
- Informed complement

The following is an **un-informed complement**. If I were to meet Tiger Woods, I could say, "Mr. Woods you are a great golfer."

The second type of complement is an **informed complement**. Using the same example, I might say, "Mr. Woods, you are a great golfer. I have been a scratch golfer for 15 years and was on the PGA tour for a short time. Your swing defines perfection. It is a pleasure watching you."

The 'informed' complement has a much greater impact on the listener. If you can make an informed complement to the person about his 'hot button', you will elevate yourself in his eyes.

How we speak with our bodies

Body Language. A great deal has been written on the subject of body language and we will not do an in-depth study of the subject. We will, however, discuss those areas of body language that you will most often encounter during the interview process.

Cannot lie with your body. It has been said that "people can lie with their lips but cannot lie with their body language." So being able to read what people are saying with their bodies is very important in the interviewing process.

Interpreting body language is not as hard as it may seem. First, understand that we all use body language to communicate. We use this in conjunction with our voices. This is a natural part of who we are and how we communicate. It is more pronounced in some people and cultures, but we all use it. In the interviewing process, you should look for several body positions and actions. For example:

Sitting upright, gathering information. In the interview, if a person is sitting upright in his chair and **leaning** forward, it indicates he is focused on what is being said. He is in the *information-gathering* mode and is forming opinions about you and your qualifications. As long as he is in this posture, you have the floor. Find an opportunity to tell one or several of your

"S.O.A.R.s." You are feeding him information that proves to him that you understand his problems. More importantly, you are showing him that you have faced these same problems in the past and can solve them again in the future.

The interviewer will often be making notes on your resume. If he does make notes, speak in simple declarative sentences. Let him digest what you say, especially the 'bottom line' of each of your "S.O.A.R.s." These are what he will often note for future reference. After you have presented a "S.O.A.R.," ask the question: "Do you find this type of information helpful?" Remember, you are not the only one he is interviewing. You want him to remember you in a positive light and his ability to take accurate notes helps this process.

Leaning back, casual conversation. If the person doing the interview is leaning back in his chair with his hands folded, you can generally assume that he is relaxed and open to casual conversation. This type of conversation is designed to evaluate you as a person. Assume his same posture and talk about his 'hot button'. He will usually maintain this position until he has made an assessment of your personality. This may take less than a minute or may be extended over the expanse of a lunch. Let the interviewer set the pace and take the lead in this. During this phase, he is finding out if you are a 'member of his tribe'.

Hands behind the head, 'I accept you'. Look for an overt body movement that says, "I accept you as a member of my tribe." This body language may be in multiple forms. In the most obvious form, the person will place his hands behind his head exposing his armpits with a big smile on his face. This is the most vulnerable position in which a person can place himself. If he does this, he is saying, "I trust you. I can work with you." A less obvious sign might be a sudden movement from the edge of the chair to the back of the chair, leaning back and smiling at the same time. Or he may move from a slouching position to an upright sitting position, again with a big smile.

When he makes the 'I accept you as a member of my tribe' sign, it is time to ask a question. The question should be rehearsed and sound like this: "Mr. Jones, I must say that I like everything I have heard and would love to join your team. Mr. Jones, how do you *feel* about my becoming part of your team?"

After you have asked the question, say nothing else and, above all, do not interrupt him while he answers the question.

The best answer he can give you is, "I have a good feeling about you." To which you will say, "Excellent, can we go to the next level and assume that I am being offered the position?" This may seem aggressive, but it is not. It shows your willingness to move forward in securing the position. The interviewer will often appreciate your candor. Either way, asking the question will establish your posture in his eyes concerning the job. It is better for him to know than to guess.

Eye movements. It has been said: "The eyes are the windows of the soul." When a person is speaking, if he looks up and to his right, generally he is recalling some fact or event from memory. If he looks down and to his left, he is constructing an answer or thinking 'out loud'. If he is looking directly into your eyes and speaking, he is generally intent on gaining your reaction to what he is saying, often looking for approval. If a person avoids looking into your eyes, he may have a self-esteem problem. If a person blinks frequently, it may be because he has contacts and his eyes are dry. If a person does not blink when he talks, it may indicate he is processing information as he is speaking. Some people do this as opposed to looking down.

Facial expressions. Facial expressions are generally the easiest to read. We learn to read facial expressions before we can talk. We know what a smile means, what a frown means, what a scowl means. We know what a question look likes. We know the look of concern. We know the look of approval. To prove my point, I suggest you watch a television show and turn off the sound. See if you can follow the story line by just watching their facial expressions. You can. If you want to really have some fun, watch a television show broadcast in another language and listen to their voice inflections while you watch their facial expressions. You will be able to understand the gist of the story. Doing this is good practice in learning how to read body language as well.

A very important note on learning to read body language: Practice, practice, practice on everybody you meet. The more you do it, the better you will be to the point that it will become automatic. You need to do this in a low stakes environment before you go to you interviews. Again, the television is very good for this.

Unreadable people. There are some people who are just unreadable. No matter what you observe, you cannot get a read on them. In this case, the only way you can know what they are thinking is to *ask*. So to this end, I suggest you memorize these sentences and practice them on your friends:

- Have I explained myself clearly?
- Is what I just said the type of information you need?
- How do you *feel* about what I have said thus far?
- Has anything I have said been of help?

Not an exact science. To conclude our discussion on body language, understand that this is not an exact science. For instance, a person who has his arms crossed generally is considered defensive or closed to the discussion. On the other hand, he may just be a little cold. Therefore, I would caution you as to making hard and fast determinations by a single posture or movement. Rather, look at all the body language and determine what he is saying using his whole body. And remember, 'the mouth can lie, but the body cannot.'

Handling objections. If the interviewer voices any objections, write them down. When he is finished, read back the list of objections one at a time and address each in a non-threatening way.

For example: "Mr. Jones, you mentioned that you felt I do not have the language skills to manage a group of Spanish speaking workers. I can see how you may have perceived that. However, I failed to mention that I studied Spanish in school and briefly attended a language school in Mexico City. Also, my wife is a bilingual teacher in the public schools. Does this paint a more accurate picture concerning my Spanish language skills?"

Another example: "Mr. Smith, you correctly mentioned that my being a new graduate, I do not have experience operating a turret lathe. However, I would mention to you that I do have extensive experience in rebuilding engines, which also requires milling various parts. The process is the same. Does this paint a more accurate picture of my skills?"

Another example: "Mr. Dole, you correctly observed that I do not have direct experience in arranging international travel. However, I would assert that the process is the same for both domestic and international. In fact, arranging international travel is somewhat easier because the profit margins are higher and there are more service agents at my disposal. I am confident of my ability to make international arrangements. Does this address your concern?

Another example: "Ms. Williams, you correctly noted that I have never worked in a high volume manufacturing area. However, I have been responsible for weekly reports, which required me to keep on top of the daily workflow in order to meet the reporting deadline. I understand the urgency of the immediate task at hand. I would feel very comfortable doing this job. Does this address your concern?"

Notice that in each example, you stated the objection, you stated a skill or accomplishment from your "S.O.A.R.s" that fit the situation, and then, most importantly, you asked the question, "Does this address your concern?"

Questions to ask at the interview.   It is very important that you ask these questions. Doing so will keep you from having to guess their answers.
- May I ask you a few questions?
- How do you *feel* about me?
- How do you *feel* about my qualifications?
- Do you *feel* my personality will fit in with your team?
- Are their any issues with which you are uncomfortable?
- Have I answered your questions to your satisfaction?
- Do you believe I am a close match to what you are looking for?
- What would be the perfect person for the job?
- Of those qualifications, which are the 3 most important?

- Why did the last person leave the position?
- Every organization assumes the personality of its leader, what is your president like?
- What do I need to do to join your team?

THE question you should NOT answer. If you are asked what you want to earn, **do not answer this question.** There are several reasons, all of which we will further discuss in Tool #13. So, how do you skirt the question, "How much do you want to make?"

How to dodge this question. There are several answers you can give. (I will warn you that you must practice giving these answers in front of someone before getting in front of the interviewer.) Here are some examples of responses to the question: "How much do you want to make?"

- "Money is, of course, important, but being fulfilled in a position is more important."
- "If we are to the point of discussing money, can I assume I have the job?"
- "I have an idea as to what this general position is paid within the industry, and I assume you are in this ball park."
- "Rather than talk about what I will cost the company, I would like to explore what I can add to the company's profit."
- "Every successful company knows 'you get what you pay for'. My value to the company will surely exceed my cost."

- "I feel sure your company is like most in that you have a predetermined salary range for this position. Will you share that with me?"
- And if all else fails:
  o "Please forgive me for not wanting to exclude myself by giving you a number that is too high or too low. I am sure that if the fit is right for both of us, the money issue can also be worked out."

Ok, the third "P", **Pacing**, has given you the tools to:

- Control how they perceive you by how you look and how you act.
- Know how to read their body language.
- Know how to address the topic of money during the interview.

If you have attended to the process, you have made a favorable impression and left with the knowledge that you ARE a 'member of their tribe.'

The fourth and final "P", **Persistence**, will be addressed in Tool # 14, but first *the topic of money*...

The Topic of MONEY

Interview paralysis. The topic of money often causes a person to become paralyzed during the interview. After all, there is a great deal at stake when it comes to what you are to be paid for your efforts. Understanding how to approach the topic of money is very important. If done properly, you will be comfortable discussing it and you will know how to effectively negotiate for the best deal.

Warning. Be forewarned, you cannot effectively discuss money 'on the fly'. You MUST know several facts before you can *intelligently* address the topic of money. To do this, you MUST do your homework and determine the following information:

- How much is required for you to maintain your standard of living?
- What is industry currently paying for the position you are interviewing?
- What do you bring to the position that equates into profit for the company?
- How to skirt the direct questions concerning money in the interview.

We will look at each of these in detail.

How much money does it take for you to live? In Tool #10, you were instructed to determine what income you need to maintain your standard of living. Why is this important?

Because to accept any amount less than what you need to maintain your living standards will automatically cause stress in your life. Knowing this dollar amount will save you the heartache of lowering your living standard or going into debt to maintain it. Lets review these instructions given in Chapter 10:

Your living expenses. First, determine how much is required for you to live; not how much you think you are worth, but rather what it costs to maintain your standard of living. If you do not know this amount, obtain your last several years' tax returns during the time you were working. Total these and divide by the number of months. For example, if you earned $48,000 in 2002 and $49,500 in 2003. This totals a gross amount of $97,500 for the 24 months. Divide this number by 24 to get an average amount per month. This equals $4,062.50 per month or $48,750.00 per year. You need to know this number before you begin any discussion of money. Why? Because this will be the least you can accept for the position. Accepting anything less will automatically add to your stress level.   Now that you know this number, DO NOT share it with anyone, especially in the interview.

What is industry currently paying for the position you are interviewing?   Do   your   homework   in determining what your skill set and experience will command in the workforce. You can do this by going onto the Internet. The Internet has a host of websites dedicated to showing the average salaries for various types of work. A simple search such on www.google.com on "average salary for carpenter" will return a host of sites that have that information. Know this before you go to the interview.

What you bring to the position that equates into profit for the company? Companies hire people with the understanding that they will *make* them money. That what they do will, in some way, add to the 'bottom line'. Hiring you is no exception. Know your 'value' before going to the interview. If you have completed your "S.O.A.R.s" properly, this has already been done. If not, rethink your accomplishments and place dollar figures beside your 'results' section.

This is true even if you are in a support role and not directly involved in producing profit. If you are interviewing for a support role, look for ways to show how what you did added to the bottom line. For example: "As an executive assistant, I was able to cut travel time for my boss by 12 days per year by advanced scheduling of his appointments. At $500 per day expenses, this saved the company $6,000 per year."

How to skirt the direct questions concerning money in the interview. (This was discussed in the previous tool, but we will repeat it here.) At some point during the interview, the topic of money will come up. If they ask you what you want to make, do not answer this question directly. **Why?**

Lets say that the job has a ceiling of $60,000. If you were to tell them you want $48,750, you would be leaving a lot of money on the table. In addition, giving them this number may tell them that you are not as valuable as they may believe you to be. On the other hand, if they were thinking the position is only worth $40,000, your $48,700 would automatically exclude you from the process.

No, it is very important that you force them to be the first to place a number on the table.

'Skirting' the question. So, how do you skirt the question, "How much do you want to make?" There are several answers you can give. (I will warn you that you must practice giving these answers in front of someone before getting in front of the interviewer.) Here are some possible answers to the question, "How much do you want to make?"

- "Money is, of course, important; however, being fulfilled in a position is more important."
- "If we are to the point of discussing money, can I assume I have the job?"
- "I have an idea as to what this general position is paid within the industry; I assume you are in this ball park?"
- "Rather than talk about what I will cost the company, I would like to explore what I can add to the company's profit."

- "Every successful company knows 'you get what you pay for'. My value to the company will surely exceed my cost."
- "I feel sure your company is like most in that they have a predetermined salary range this position. Will you share that with me?"
- And if all else fails:
  o "Please forgive me for not wanting to exclude myself by giving you a number that is too high or too low. I am sure that if the fit is right for both of us, the money issue can also be worked out."

If the job is a fit for you, and they want you, but the money is too low, consider this approach:

- "Tom, I want to join your team and know I could be a vital part of making the company's dream a reality. However, please understand that the salary you are discussing will not cover my living expenses. Could we perhaps discuss possibly expanding my responsibilities to justify an additional 8%?"

Notice the approach. You expressed to them:
- Your desire to join the team.
- An honest answer concerning your living expenses.
- A tangible number for additional salary that he can take to management.

You now know how to address the topic of money during the interview. Now, practice, practice, practice.

Last resort. If they insist you make the first offer, you can say something like: "My research has indicated that the position I am being offered has an industry range of between $45,000 and $56,500. This comes from the Department of Labor and is regionalized. I have the details if you choose to see them. Understanding that 'you get what you pay for', I can only assume that you will be willing to pay within this range. My expenses are approximately $49,500 per year. Therefore, I believe a good match for both the company's interests and my own objectives would be $54,750 per year. This would meet my requirements and I hope yours. How does this sound to you?"

"It has been said that the *love* of money is the root of all evil. The *want* of money is so quite as truly."
                              -Samuel Butler (1835-1902)
                              English author and philosopher

Tool #14

Persistence

OK, you have **Prepared** for the interview; you have made an impressive **Presentation** by how you look, you have distinguished yourself through **Pacing** in the actual face-to-face interviews. Our final "P" in the interview process is for **Persistence**, or *"What to do after you leave the interview..."*

The issue of persistence takes on several 'out of the box' activities. The first and foremost activity should be to send handwritten 'thank you' notes to everyone with whom you have met. Not an email, but an 'old-fashioned' thank you note like the one on the following page.

An 'Old-Fashioned' Thank You Note

Notice the construction of this note: "Tom, Just a quick note to say thank you for meeting with me yesterday. I would love to join your team." Sign it and put a thumbprint. Include your business card or if you do not have a business card, a phone number.

Thumb print? Why a thumbprint? Placing a thumbprint makes this thank you note memorable by making it even more personal. Placing your thumbprint on the card makes it a 'high touch' piece of communication. It is so unusual that the person will remember you because of the novelty of it. Try it and you will be surprised at the responses you will receive.

Mail it the same day. It is imperative that you send the thank you note on the same day of your interview. The sooner they get the thank you note, the better you look. To make an even greater impression, hand deliver it to the office and leave it at the front desk for delivery to the person. It all makes a statement.

Potential networking contact. There is another very important reason for the thank you note. Even if you do *not* get the job, you have a potential networking contact that you can use in the future (We discuss this in detail in the section on *PowerNetworking*). Do not miss any opportunity to network with someone in your industry, especially decision makers.

'Mentally' take the job. Another 'out of the box' approach is to consider 'mentally' taking the job for which you have applied. Start to think how you would do the job if you had it. This effort in **P**ersistence will enable you to contact the decision maker with a follow up phone call saying something like this, "Mr. Smith, this is Barry Vanek, do you have a minute? Mr. Smith, I could not stop thinking about our discussion during my interview. I would like to run a few ideas before you concerning the inventory shrinkage. I had a very similar problem a few years ago and I think I may have a new twist on how to solve the problem. May I come see you tomorrow at 2:00?"

Devote your ideas to paper. Another 'out of the box' approach is to devote your ideas to paper and make a call something like this, "Mr. Smith, this is Barry Vanek, do you have a minute? Mr. Smith, I could not stop thinking about the topics we discussed during my interview. I would like to run a few ideas in front of you concerning the inventory shrinkage. I had a very similar problem a few years ago and I think I may have a new twist on how to solve the problem. I have documented my thoughts and developed a 5-page document on the subject. I would really like to discuss it with you. May I come see you tomorrow at 2:00?"

Volunteer to work for free. Another 'out of the box' approach reads like this: "Mr. Smith, this is Barry Vanek, do you have a minute? Mr. Smith, I just have to tell you that I am excited at even the prospect of joining your team. In fact, I am so excited about the position that I will volunteer to work for 2 weeks for free in order to show you that I can be an asset to your group. With your permission, I can start today."

Enthusiasm is contagious. A word here about enthusiasm: *Enthusiasm is contagious.* Always has been - always will be. If you find any opportunity to show enthusiasm, *do it.* The interview process is not the time to be 'cool'. It is the time to show that you want the job and you can solve their problems with gusto and enthusiasm. Very few people are enthusiastic and those that are stand out in people's minds.

"A man can succeed at almost anything for which he has unlimited enthusiasm."
-Charles Schwab (1862-1939)
American steel magnate

I hope you see how these 'out of the box' approaches will distinguish you from your competition.

Never stop networking. The last item in **Persistence** is wrapped up in the word 'network'. Whether or not you get the job, consider each person with whom you interviewed as a potential part for your network. What do you mean, part of my network? In this brave new world in which we now live, job security is quickly fading. We counsel clients by impressing upon them 2 very important situations under the 'new rules'. First rule is 'the company has no soul'. This means that it will let you go for any reason to make the bottom line look better. Second, from here forward, consider your present job as lasting only 2 years. And so, if you will be changing jobs every 2 years, it is very important to never stop networking.

To this end, make it a point to contact every decision maker with whom you meet, twice a year just to 'keep in touch'. He will be in your network and you will be in his. How do you do this? Simple.

Call Mr. Smith and say, "Mr. Smith, I am very disappointed that I did not get the job, but I do understand. Mr. Smith, I have a favor to ask, may I call you a couple of times each year just to keep in touch? With the way things are in the job market, networking is very important. Who knows, maybe I can be of help to you is some way."

Now, a final word concerning the entire interview process: You may have done all 4 of your P's 100% correct and you still do not get the job. It has happened to us all. If this is the case, remember 3 very important things:
- First, you have done all that you could, physically and emotionally. Take pride in the fact that everything you *could* do, you *did* do.

- Second, understand that there are a host of things that you cannot control. At the top of this list is who gets the job. For example, everyone has heard the story of the job going to the president's unqualified nephew.
- Third, remember that each time you go through this process, you get better at it. You get smoother delivering your "S.O.A.R.s," more confident in your pacing, smarter at reading the other person's body language. Consider each interview as an opportunity to hone your skills. These are skills that will serve you in your new job as well as the rest of your life.

You are now equipped to interview like a professional. You know how to:

- **Prepare** for the interview.
- **Present** yourself by looking like a professional.
- **Pace** the person so as to become "A Member of Their Tribe."
- **Persist** in the process even after the interview is over.

With these tools in your toolbox, you are now worlds ahead of your competition.

"Enthusiasm...the sustaining power of all great action."
-Samuel Smiles (1812-1904)
Scottish writer

"Enthusiasm is the inspiration of everything great. Without it no man is to be feared, and with it none despised."
-Bovee (1820-1904)
American author and editor

"Nothing is so contagious as enthusiasm; it moves stones, it charms brutes. Enthusiasm is the genius of sincerity, and truth accomplishes no victories without it."
-Bulwer-Lytton (1803-1873)
English novelist and poet

Brave New World, Brave New Rules

In this **Brave New World**, the rules have changed. Job security, as we have known it in the past, is no more. It has vanished with corporate mergers, off shore labor, downsizing and hostile takeovers. There is still job security, but it plays by *different rules*. And if you try to play by the old rules, you will lose every time. Therefore, if you truly want security in your job and your career, you must learn the new rules and play by them.

The Brave New Rules:
1. **The company has no soul.**
2. **If you have a job for 2 years, consider it long term.**

No soul. The company has no soul? No, it does not. The company will lay you off in a heartbeat if it will make its quarterly numbers look better or if expenses need to be cut for the boss to get his bonus. Now that you know this fact of life, you can function within the new rules. You can play the game and win.

You can create you own career regardless of your age, education, background, or profession.

How to function in a soul-less company.

Invest no emotional energy. When you get your next job, realize that the company has no feelings toward you, either positive or negative. Remember it has no soul, so it has no feelings. This mandates that you do **NOT invest any emotional energy in the company.** This does not mean you should not work hard. On the contrary, you are to do the absolute best job you can because it is the right thing to do and you will need to demonstrate to your next employer that you can do a good job.   But never think that the company will sacrifice on your behalf because you sacrificed for it. Remember, *the company has no soul.*

Bitter pill. This can be a bitter pill to swallow. To help ease the pain, it will be good for you to realize that your job is *not* like a marriage, for better or for worse. No, it is a business arrangement that settles the accounts every payday. The company pays you what it said it would for the work you agreed to do. They owe you nothing. You have been paid. The pay period starts the process all over again.

Change jobs every two years? Gone are the days of 35 years with a company and retirement with a pension and gold watch. Even companies that had a policy of not laying-off workers, have begun doing so. IBM is an example. Being laid-off after only 2 years is a very real possibility. This being the case, it is imperative that you *continually look for your next position.*   Start preparing your exit strategy as soon as you begin your new job. This may sound crass at first, but it is not. It is realistic.   Working for this new company will provide you with new "S.O.A.R.s," which you will use to land your next position.... with higher pay and even greater benefits.

Continually build your network. If you are going to be changing jobs every two years, you must continually build your network of people. That is what *PowerNetworking* is all about.   Creating a network of people who can propel your career. In this way you will never again be at the mercy of the company; rather you will leave on your timetable and move to higher ground in the job market.

Once you learn how to create and maintain your *PowerNetwork,* you will never be lacking for career opportunities. You will propel your career on your terms. You will never lack for a job. You will never lack for the income to support your family. You *will* live your dream.

No more 'flat-feet'. You can make this happen and never again be caught 'flat footed' by life's circumstances. You will never again be at the mercy of the 'system' for your next job. You will never again lower your income just to go back to work. You will never again struggle to 'make ends meet'.

A New Part-Time Job

It is not uncommon for people to have a second, part-time job. Usually it pays much less than you would like. What if you could have a part-time job that was fun, rewarding and paid you exceptionally well? What if this part-time job could be done any time and any place you wanted to do it? What if this part-time job had nothing to do with asking for money or selling a product? And what if this part-time job was guaranteed to make you feel good about yourself? Would you take a part-time job like this? Of course, you would. Where do you sign up? The answer is in the next Tool....

The *New* Job Security

The OLD job security model. There was a time when job security was earned. It was earned by getting a good education and by working hard for the company. It was earned by sacrificing for the company and by putting their needs above your own. Doing this would insure you of being taken care of by the company just like a mother cares for her child. No matter how bad things got, your sacrifices would earn you the security you wanted. Sad to say, it is not that way any more.

The company has no soul. As we learned in the previous Tool, the company has no soul. You are merely a number to be used and discarded at the whim of the accounting department. The reality of this fact needs to be embraced, so that you can function within the new rules. The reality is that your emotional investment in the company will not be reciprocated. There is no job security in doing that, so don't.

The NEW job security. There *is* security in the job market. There is the ability to never be without work, to never be lacking for opportunities to move up, to advance your career and your income. You can never again be at the mercy of the 'system' for your next job and never again lower your income just to go back to work. You will never again struggle to 'make ends meet'. Yes, there *is* this kind of security.

This NEW job security looks and acts differently from its predecessor. It has different rules, different methods, and different outcomes. This new job security is defined by a single word, *PowerNetworking*.

First, what is networking?   Networking may be defined as: *"Developing a broad list of contacts -- people you've met through various social and business functions -- and encouraging them to assist you in looking for a job. People in your network may be able to give you job leads, offer you advice and information about a particular company or industry, and introduce you to others so that you can expand your network."*

This definition is the traditional definition of networking. It is a working definition of what it means to network for the purpose of finding a job. It clearly shows that it is important to meet people who can help you in your job search. It is obvious that if we meet the right people, we stand a better chance of getting a job. It also alludes to the fact that these contacts can support us in our careers after our job search has resulted in securing a new job.

Everyone networks. The truth is, we all network. You may say, "I don't network." *Yes, you do*. Everyone networks to varying degrees. For example, 20% of the people in this country move each year. When these people move, they must establish new relationships. They must meet new realtors. They must meet new school officials and teachers, new neighbors, new baby sitters, new mechanics, co-workers. The list goes on and on. You may or may not have moved recently, but there is a good chance you have met someone who has. This is networking. Lets be candid; we all need the goods and services others provide. It has been accurately said that 'no man is an island'. We truly need each other. Establishing and developing these relationships is called networking.

Why do some people have great networks and others don't?

Ted Turner and CNN

Ted Turner, the CEO of Turner Broadcasting gambled on a 24-hour cable news program. Ted had developed a relationship with a sheik of the Royal Family in the Middle East who owned a hotel in Kuwait. When the war broke out in the Middle East, all of the journalists were asked to leave with the exception of Ted Turner's news crew. The Sheik granted him permission to stay in his hotel and said they would be protected. Throughout the first Gulf War, CNN broadcast real-time war events and placed Ted Turner at the forefront of the new industry.

Had Ted not networked with the Sheik, he would not now be a household word.

Bill Gates and Microsoft

When the personal computer was first being introduced into the marketplace, there were 2 major computer software operating systems: CP/M and MSDOS. Bill Gates had purchased an operating system for $50,000, which he named MSDOS (Micro Soft Disk Operating System). *(An operating system is the software that logically connects all the hardware in the computer, such as monitor, keyboard, memory, hard drives, etc. Each computer must have an operating system in order to operate.)* The CP/M operating system was clearly superior to MSDOS in just about every respect. Gates then went to the product manager of IBM who was in charge of what IBM called the "Hobby Box": The IBM Personal Computer (IBM PC). Bill sold his MSDOS operating system to IBM for $50 a copy. CP/M was selling for $200 a copy. IBM signed with Microsoft to supply the operating system for its PC. This, then, became the accepted standard for PC operating systems.

The owner of CP/M could have done the same thing, but he did not. Bill Gates was the one who purposed to meet the key individuals to sell his product. At the time he was a young college drop out. Had Bill Gates not networked with the product manager at IBM, we would not know him today as the richest man in the world.

The list goes on and on. Each successful and prominent person got where he is because of his network. Famous people such as Arnold Schwarzenegger, Oprah, Sylvester Stallone, and others all are where they are today not because of their talent, but *because of their networks*.

Your network is your job security. You must accept the fact that your career depends first and foremost on your network.   Not your education, not your experience, not your credentials, but your network. Your network will be THE single greatest factor in the success of your career.

This is very good news. Why is this good news? Because you and you alone have direct control over your network. You can meet targeted people who can energize your career.   You can do this.   And the following chapters will give you the Tools necessary to create this network.

Money in the bank. We invest our money in such a way that it will earn interest. We can also invest our time in the same way. How we invest what we do each day will determine what gains we receive. *PowerNetworking* is a wise investment in your time and efforts, greater than any bank or investment portfolio can produce.   In Tool #17, you will discover the difference between networking and *PowerNetworking*.

"Friendship is the only cement that will ever hold the world together. "

-Woodrow Wilson (1856-1924)
28th American President

"Friends are as companions on a journey, who ought to aid each other to persevere in the road to a happier life."

-Pythagoras (B.C. 582-507)
Greek philosopher and mathmician

Networking vs.
PowerNetworking

"80% of life is just showing up."

-Woody Allen

"80% of life is just showing up..." may be true; however, the *success* in life lies in what you do with the other 20% *after you show up.* It is this 20% we will be exploring for the remainder of this book. We will uncover the secrets of success as evidenced by successful people. We will learn how to be proactive in our efforts to meet people and cultivate relationships that make a difference...a difference now and throughout our lives.

Who you know... We have all heard the phrase: "It's not *What* you know, but *Who* you know." Truer words have never been spoken. And there is a variation that is even more true:

"It's not What you know,
It's not Who you know...
It's <u>**WHO KNOWS YOU!!!**</u>"

There is a difference in networks. Not all networks are the same. The 'Who' you know is the focus of the traditional network. The '*Who knows you*' is the focus of a *PowerNetwork* that can make all the difference in your life.

There is a difference in these two types of networks. Just knowing a lot of people does not insure your success. It is *who knows you* and looks out for your best interests that defines a network that is powerful enough to propel your career. Powerful enough command your attention. Powerful enough to be cared for and nurtured. This type of network deserves a new name: a name that will distinguish itself from the traditional network.

A *New* Name for a *New* Network. Any tool that is as powerful as the network you are about to discover needs a new name. A name that signifies what it does for you and for others. That name is *PowerNetwork*.

PowerNetworking is the *New* Job Security

The difference between networking and *PowerNetworking.* Networking is simply knowing a host of people. *PowerNetworking* is much different. *PowerNetworking* has a set of objectives, which sets it apart from the traditional network. *PowerNetworking* calls upon several very basic human emotions, as well as psychological principles, which motivate us as humans.   These   motivations   are   at   the   core   of *PowerNetworking*.

Your new part-time job.   As an introduction to the remainder of this book, *PowerNetworking* covers a specific list of things that must be done to create and maintain a *PowerNetwork*.   These are each highlighted as a specific tool for your toolbox.   Each adds value to your *PowerNetwork*.   Each of these tools is a complete activity unto itself.   However, together they become the basis of a *PowerNetwork*.   When you make the quality decision to make building a *PowerNetwork* your continuing part-time job, you have just turned the corner of life onto the road named 'Success'.

"The secret of all victory lies in the organization of the non-obvious."

-Spengler (1880-1936)

"I can give you a six-word formula for success:
Think things through - then follow through."

-Edward Rickenbacker (1890-1973)

Tool #18

S.M.A.R.T. Goals

"The superior man perseveres long in his course, adapts to the times, but remains firm in his direction and correct in his goals."

-I Ching (1550 BC?)

Goals can take us where our spirit wants us to be. There is great power in setting goals. There is strength beyond ourselves that is called upon when we set goals. There is great achieving with great goals. There is a future for those who learn the power at their disposal in setting goals. There is job security to those brave enough to set goals. And it is job security that we truly want. So, lets learn just how goals work and how to make use of this very important Tool.

Goals. By definition, successful goals are S.M.A.R.T. S.M.A.R. T. is an acronym for:

- **S**pecific
- **M**easurable
- **A**ttainable
- **R**elevant
- **T**ime bound

Dennis Waitley correctly stated, "Winners can tell you where they are going, what they plan to do along the way, and who will be sharing the adventure with them."

Goals that are S.M.A.R.T. will become reality. Successful people know this. People such as:

- Stephen Covey, who wrote *7 Habits of Highly Effective People,*
- Charles Schwab, who started a national discount brokerage firm, and
- Dale Carnegie, who wrote *How to Win Friends and Influence People.*

All of these people learned the power of S.M.A.R.T. goals. They know the power contained in these goals and how to make them a reality. They know that in order for a goal to be reached, it must be S.M.A.R.T. and it must be in writing.

In the case of *PowerNetworking*, let us all adopt the following goal:

"Within 2 years, *I will*: create and maintain a *PowerNetwork* of 24 quality people. These people will enable me to succeed in all areas of my life. I will also be an integral part of helping each of these individuals succeed in his efforts. Within this *PowerNetwork*, I will have at least 2 mentors and become a mentor for at least 2."

To become a valid goal, it is imperative that you write this goal down. I encourage you to get a 3-ring binder and title it your *'PowerNetworking* Toolbox'. On page 1 write the above goal.

Now that you have written your goal, lets look at it closely. The most important words in your goal are the words:

"I will..."

When you commit these words to any issue in your life, you unleash power that will astound you. You will be shocked at what will happen to you and around you when you make a quality decision beginning with the words, "I will..."

Quality Decision. It is important to understand what a quality decision is. Most people in life never make quality decisions. They make decisions, but they always have a way 'out'. They are always noncommittal to the point that if it doesn't work out like they planned, they do not 'lose face'. People who make these types of decisions are mostly 're-active' when it comes to life. They make decisions based on what is happening to them at that moment. They spend their life in anticipation of what may happen to them next and hope to avoid the pitfalls. Life seems to continually 'slap' them in the face and they become more and more cynical about life as they get older. At the end of their lives, they are bitter about everything. We all know people like this.

Pro-active about life. As a contrast, there are some people who are not 're-active' when it comes to life. No, they are *pro-active*. They make life happen on their terms, not the world's terms. They are the ones who have smiles on their faces. They have a song in their voices and they exude confidence. You know the type. These are the people you want to be around. When you are in their presence, you believe anything is possible. You do not think about your problems, you think about your *possibilities*. These are the people who have learned to make quality decisions.

So how do you make a quality decision? Quality decisions take three separate and distinct actions:
- First, your quality decision MUST be written down.
- Second, your quality decision must be S.M.A.R.T. (specific, measurable, attainable, relevant, and time bound).
- Third, you must place a written copy of your quality decision/goal where you can see it everyday.
- Fourth, you must read your quality decision/goal everyday.

Once you have done these 4 things, you have started the process of making a quality decision. The operative word is 'started'. Why just started?

After you do the four steps, your mind will accept the decision, but it may take some time for the decision to be imbedded within your soul. Your soul is the inner *you*, the 'who YOU are' part of you. It is what comes out when you are under pressure. When the stress of life beats all the façade from your personality and there is nothing left but you and your back against the wall. This is the part that is ready to dig in and fight for what you know is right. This is your soul. Once this decision reaches and changes your soul, THEN it becomes a quality decision.

Great peace follows a quality decision.

There is great peace that accompanies the experience. This is a peace that will tell your mind, "I don't care what I see; I only care what I *believe*." This peace will enable you to laugh at life, knowing that you will come out on top.

Rare indeed are those who make quality decisions. But you now have the tools in your toolbox to make it happen. So, as the Nike commercial says, "Just DO It!!!"

Next, let us explore the next phrase in our S.M.A.R.T. Goal:

"...create and maintain a *PowerNetwork* of 24 quality people. These people will enable me to succeed in all areas of my life. I will also be an integral part of helping each of these individuals succeed in his efforts."

"24 people...I know a lot more than 24 people," you may say, and you are correct. But understand that

we are building a *PowerNetwork*, not just a network. To be a *PowerNetwork* contact they must meet 2 criteria:
1. **You must add value to their lives in some way.**
2. **They must add value to your life in some way.**

It cannot be a one-way street. You cannot just use people to further your own ends. If you do, you will eventually find yourself out of friends and will also earn the reputation of someone who only 'takes' and never 'gives'. Not a good reputation to have.

Key to your success. No, *PowerNetwork* contacts are those whom you can help and those who can help you. These *PowerNetwork* contacts are the key to your success. These are the people who will support you in your career. More importantly, you will be a support for them in their career. Furthermore, these will be the people who will continually be looking out for ways to assist you and make your life better. They will also be looking for people to whom they can introduce you. And you will be doing the same.

Bottom line concerning building a *PowerNetwork*:

PowerNetworking is not about YOU!!!
It is about THEM!!!

PowerNetworking is about you helping *them* succeed. It is about using your contacts, resources, experiences, and personality to actively *help* them succeed.

Here   is   the   driving   engine   behind
PowerNetworking:

"What goes around...
comes around."

WHAT???   Yes, "What goes around...comes
around." If you have lived any time at all, you know
this to be true. Whatever we dish out to others will
always come back to you. This includes the bad things
*as **well as the good things**.*

"Whatsoever good thing any man doeth, the same shall he
receive from the Lord, whether he be bond or free."
                    -King James Holy Bible, Ephesians 6:8

If you make it your quest to help people in their
efforts, you will find that there will be people that will
help you in your efforts. If you do not believe this to be
true, try this experiment: As you are driving, look for
opportunities to allow other drivers to pull into your
lane. When they indicate that they need or want to get
in front of you, LET THEM. After you begin doing this,
notice how easy it is to find someone who will allow
you to move into his or her lane.   You will be shocked.
This works as long as you are the one to initiate the
action. *If you give unselfishly, you will be given to
unselfishly.* What goes around... comes around.

Warning... Don't do your good deeds for the expressed purpose of having that person return the favor. If you do this, you are missing the point. You do favors for people who need your help and you *do not keep a tally sheet* on who owes whom. Actively look for ways to help others without expecting a returned favor of any kind and you will be shocked at the number of people who will seek you out in order to help you. It will not necessarily be the one that you helped, however.

This is the essence of *PowerNetworking*: doing for others and allowing others to do for you.

Important People Called Mentors

Life is a journey. On your journey, there are people who have already *gone* where you want to go. In addition, there are people who want to go where you have already *been*. While you are developing your *PowerNetwork*, look for both of these individuals. These people fall into the *mentor* category. These are the single most valuable people you can have in your *PowerNetwork*. When you find these people, you are worlds ahead of most. Why?

Having a Mentor. A true mentor will allow you to express your dreams, ideas, and activities and then tell you if you are on the path to success or failure. They know because they have been there. And you can fulfill the same role for someone else. You can counsel someone who is following your path through life.

Helping them succeed is pivotal to your success as a person of honor, integrity, and stature.

Being a Mentor. There are people who want to go where you have been. They want to know what you know. They need the advantage of your wisdom in order to know what to do and what not to do. They want someone who will not judge them, but rather will encourage them. They want a person who will stand by them when they fail and help them succeed. These people are out there, right under your nose.

So how do you find a mentor and a person *to* mentor? The answer to this question is as simple as the nose on your face. In fact, the answer is the nose on your face. These people are literally under your nose. What?? Yes, you see these people all the time and just do not recognize them for who they are: mentors or people to be mentored. So why don't you see them? Because you are not looking for them. Let me illustrate:

Your new car. Have you ever bought a car? If you are like most people, you shopped around and made an emotional decision (backed up with facts) on a particular make and model of car. Once you had this clearly in your thinking, you saw this same car everywhere you looked. They were all over the place. Why had you not seen them before? *Because you were not looking for them before.* It is the same with mentors, *PowerNetworking* contacts, watches, houses, books...you name it, anything you really want, you will begin to 'spot'.

If you do not believe this is true, answer the next few questions. For this test, you will assume that you will be given the car of your choosing. No cost to you, absolutely free. Now complete the form with this fantasy in mind.

Your FREE Dream Car:
Make:_____
Model:_____
Color:_____
Accessories:_____

Now that you clearly have this vehicle in mind, notice how often you see this exact same car or one very close. You will be shocked.

Another Example:

Years ago, while vacationing with our young children, we would play a game while driving. The game was finding license plates from all 50 states. The game involved the entire family and was great fun. And to everyone's surprise, we DID find all 50 states, including Rhode Island, Alaska, and *Hawaii*. We saw them everywhere: parking lots, highways, and roadsides. Wherever we went we were always looking at license plates. (As a side note, we found the greatest variety of license plates in the National Parks parking lots.) We were actually successful in finding all 50 states during our 2-week vacation.

Whatever you seek...you will find. The point is that if you make the quality decision to find something, you will.

Summary.   As   a   summary   on   goals   and *PowerNetworking*, all great people operate with goals. I would say to you that they are not great just by chance. They are just ordinary people with extraordinary goals. If you want to make your life better, for yourself and your family, you must have goals.

"Aim high and you will land high."

"Never take aim and you will never hit the target."

"You will never soar with eagles if you are spending your time just peckin' round in the dirt."

                                                            -Unknown

Your Reach

Your reach is farther than you think. Here is a little known fact:

You are only 6 people away
from anyone in the world.

This includes the President of the United States or the Premier of China. This is to say:

you know someone...
who knows someone...
who knows someone...
who knows someone...
who knows someone...
who knows the President or the Premier.

How is this possible? On the average, everyone knows and interfaces with approximately 200 people (the actual average being 223). This means that if you could meet each of the 200 people each of *your* 200 contacts knows, you would have met 40,000 people (200 X 200=40,000).

One degree. Stated another way, you are 'one degree' away from 40,000 people. That is a lot of people and they are all just *one person away from you*. Remember, each person you know also knows approximately 200 people.

The big question. Now, this begs a question: Of the 40,000 people that are just one degree away from you, do you think there is *one that can offer you a job*?

The bigger answer. The obvious answer is YES!!! Your success is quite possibly as close as your existing network.

8 million people. But wait, lets examine this line of reasoning a bit farther. Lets take it just one degree farther: if you could be introduced to each of these 40,000 individual's 200 contacts, you would be introduced to *8 million people*! This is only 2 degrees away. Three degrees puts your reach up to *1.6 billion people*, and 4 degrees, *320 billion*. This means that you have potential contacts, if managed properly, *with everyone who could insure your success*. And that, my reading friend, equals JOB SECURITY.

We are a connected society. Think about this for a moment: you are one degree away from 40,000 people and 2 degrees away from 8 million people. We truly are a connected society. Now, ask yourself the question, "Are there 24 people, among the 40,000 who are separated by one person, who can make up my *PowerNetwork*?" Again, the obvious answer is, "YES!!!"

And they are just 1 degree away from you. Therefore, you are only 1 degree away from your success.

This connectivity with others is called your 'reach' and it is at your disposal. You have access to 40,000 people who are directly in contact with your immediate contacts. This is awesome. Dwell on this until it sinks in and becomes part of your thinking.

A book that explores this concept in depth is <u>Six Degrees: The Science of A Connected Age</u> by Duncan J. Watts. This book is excellent reading and worthy of your attention if you are the type who wants to know 'why things work the way they do.'

Your reach, your future. Your reach enables you to meet those people who will find you a job, who will propel your career, and who will insure your job security. This is *your* reach and knowing how to 'work' your reach is what the remainder of this book is about.

"A friend is, as it were, a second self.

-Cicero (B.C. 106-43)

Pick and Shovel Work

Nothing worth having is free or easy. Creating your *PowerNetwork* is no exception. The act of creating your *PowerNetwork* will take some effort. In fact, it may take a great deal of effort for some of you; but trust me, it will be worth it. This laborious 'pick and shovel' work only has to be done once and the rest is easy. So be prepared to spend whatever time it takes. Remember, the quality decision to do so means the task is virtually complete; the rest is just a matter of your time. So let us begin:

Make your
PowerNetwork list

Make a *PowerNetwork* out of your list of names. Before you begin with your 'pick and shovel' work, lets again review our S.M.A.R.T. goal:

'Within 2 years, *I will*: create and maintain a *PowerNetwork* of 24 quality people. These people will enable me to succeed in all areas of my life. I will also be an integral part of helping each of these individuals succeed in their efforts. Within this *PowerNetwork*, I will have at least 2 mentors and become a mentor for at least 2.'

With these objectives clearly in mind, you will start by logically listing all of the people you currently know.

Make a list of whom you know. In order to assure a complete listing of all the people you know, I have developed 2 systems:
1. A paper-based system using a form such as Figure 20A.
2. A computer program called *PowerNet*, which is included with this book.

"No one reaches a high position without daring.
                    -Publilius Syrus (fl. B.C. 42) Roman writer

Paper system. Both systems work in essentially the same way. The paper system uses single sheets of paper for each contact whereas the computer program does this electronically. If you do not have access to a computer or simply feel more comfortable using the conventional paper method, the Figure 20A form will serve you well. There is a little more work involved, but the end result is still the same.

***PowerNet* computer program.** If you choose to use the *PowerNet* program, the instructions are included on the program itself. A generic set of instructions is also included in Appendix B. Because all computer programs go through various revisions and improvements, consider the features and instructions as rudimentary. The actual up-to-date features and instructions are contained in the newest release. For additional information, please check my web site www.GetAJob.ws.

Make initial list of contacts. Lets begin by making logical lists of all the people you currently know. Be prepared, this list will be a lot larger than you think. To create this list, begin by listing major groupings of individuals. If you choose to use the *PowerNet* program, which is included with this book, you will put this information directly into the program. If you choose to use the paper-based system, by using the Figures 20A/B forms, you can copy these, print one on front and one on back of each page, and enlarge them to 8 1/2 by 11 to be filed in a three-ring binder.

PowerNetworking

First name_____**Last name**_____[ ]Mr.[ ]Mrs.[ ]Ms.
Company Name_____ _____
Title/function_____ Birthday___/___/_____
            Contact every [ ]30 days [ ]60 days [ ]90 days [ ]120 days [ ]Yearly

Address:
[ ]Personal [ ]Business [ ]_____   Business card
Street_____
City _____State____Zip_____
[ ]Personal [ ]Business [ ]_____
Street_____
City _____State____Zip_____
[ ]Personal [ ]Business [ ]_____
Street_____
City _____State____Zip_____

Phone (___)____-_____[ ]Home [ ]Bus. [ ]Fax [ ]Cell
Phone (___)____-_____[ ]Home [ ]Bus. [ ]Fax [ ]Cell
Phone (___)____-_____[ ]Home [ ]Bus. [ ]Fax [ ]Cell
Phone (___)____-_____[ ]Home [ ]Bus. [ ]Fax [ ]Cell

Email:
_____@_____._____[ ]Personal [ ]Bus.
_____@_____._____[ ]Personal [ ]Bus.
_____@_____._____[ ]Personal [ ]Bus.
_____@_____._____[ ]Personal [ ]Bus.

Identity:
Who they **are**_____
_____
What they **do** _____
_____
What they **like**_____
_____

(Figure 20A)

Job Campaign Communications Log

Company name _____ Phone _____

Address _____ Fax _____

City/St _____ Website _____

Current notes on the company: _____

_____

Decision makers:

Name	Title	Phone	Email	Misc

Communications log:

Date	Spoke to	Action/information/directive/follow up
__/__		
__/__		
__/__		
__/__		
__/__		
__/__		
__/__		
__/__		
__/__		
__/__		
__/__		
__/__		
__/__		
__/__		
__/__		
__/__		
__/__		

(Figure 20B)

The *PowerNetwork* contact form. Lets look closely at the form. You will be filling out enough information on each person you know in order to contact them. You will also include additional information which will come in handy a little later.

1. At the top, you see lines to fill in for his name, first and last.
2. Next, are his company affiliation with title and function within the company.
3. This is followed by a very important piece of information: his birthday. Ask for his birthday. We will discuss why later.
4. Next, are the various addresses. Mark either personal or business.
5. This is followed by various phone numbers and email addresses people have. Check the appropriate box for each phone number and email address.
6. Last, you will see a section marked Identity. This is where you will answer the questions:

> **Who they *are*...**
> **What they *do*...**
> **And what they *like*...**

> ## *The Identity of the person is at the heart of PowerNetworking.*

What is an Identity? Every person is unique. Every person has qualities and attributes that make up his personality both on a business and personal level. As a *PowerNetworker*, you need to know as much about the person as you can. You do this by obtaining the details of who they are, what they do, and what they like.

Identity: Who they Are... Let's start by completing *Who they Are*. You do this by asking the following questions:
- Are they a family member; if so how are they related?
- Are they alumni from a school you attended?
- Are they a neighbor; if so where and when?
- Are they a business contact? If so, are they a vendor, customer, co-worker, or colleague?
- Are they a 'not for profit' contact? Such as religious groups, social club, political party, country club.
- Are they a sports or hobby connection? Such as golf, tennis, boating, fishing, hunting.
- Are they a personal services connection? Such as your doctor, babysitter, plumber, cleaners.
- What are their training and/or education?

Identity: What they Do... Next you will document *What they Do*.
- What is their profession?
- What are their skills?
- What field do they work in?
- What field have they worked in?
- What position do they currently have?

Identity: What they Like... Next you will document *What they Like*.
- What are their hobbies?

- What do they enjoy doing in their free time?
- What are their hot buttons?

It is important that you obtain this information from each of your contacts. You will learn how to obtain this information a little later. The more of these details you can obtain, the more effective your *PowerNetwork* becomes. It is important to track your communications with each contact. Use the back of the form to log when you contacted them and what you discussed

Let us begin the process.

You will be using one form per person. File them alphabetically. To help you list all the people you know, list them by logical groupings. This will insure that you list them all.

Group #1 Family. The first major group is your family. Both close relatives and distant relatives. List each and their relationship to you.

Group #2 Neighbors. List any current and past neighbors.

Group #3 School. This is a list of people you know **from school**. Include high school, college, and tech school, all the people you met while in school. This is where you will include any societies, clubs or fraternities/sororities friends.

Group #4 Business. Divide these between customers, vendors, colleagues, and co/workers. This is most easily done by creating stacks of business cards. A stack for customers, another stack for vendors, another stack for co-workers and so forth.

Group #5 Not for Profit. These are the people you know from church, civic clubs, social clubs, country clubs, hospitals, volunteer work and the like. If you can obtain a directory of members, get it and highlight the people you know.

Group #6 Personal Services. These are the persons you know who serve you at restaurants. Who work on your car, clean your clothes, do your housework, sell you insurance, paint your house, and do your lawn. I think you get the picture.

Group #7 Leisure Time. This includes any sports, any hobbies, anything not work related.

Give yourself time. Give yourself plenty of time for this project. In fact make this at least a 2-3 day project. You will remember names the second and third day that you did not recall on the first day. Do not begin listing names in a new group until you have exhausted the names in the previous group. If you are like most people, you should have between 125 and 300 names, the average being 228 names.

Added bonus. As an added benefit, once you complete this list, you will have an accurate listing of your entire network along with all of the contact information for each. This personal 'phone directory' can be downloaded to your PDA if you use the computer program *PowerNet.*

Now this is hard work so pace yourself. Don't quit until you have finished. Once you do, reward yourself. Eat ice cream.... you deserve it.

OK. After you have this list, you have the beginnings of a *PowerNetwork.* You're not there yet, but you have made the important first step.

PowerNet **Software instructions.**   The software replaces the paper system with the computer. The computer also automates many of the reminder and calendar functions and 'connect-the-dots' program.

Before we begin inputting data into the computer, we must explain the design physiology of the program itself. *PowerNet* was designed to be 'Simple, Useful and Powerful.'
- **Simple.** *PowerNet* does not burden you down with a host of features you'll never use. This program is designed solely for the purpose of networking. It is not a do-all-things database. It is specific in its function of building and fostering your personal network.
- **Useful.** *PowerNet* is designed so that it is a valued tool to be used on a daily basis
- **Powerful.** *PowerNet* is designed to be powerful in its ability to 'connect-the-dots', which is where the real value of your network lies.

How it works. *PowerNet* tracks each person by his or her name. It also creates an 'Identity' for each person. This 'Identity' will allow the computer to make logical associations between persons. For instance, this 'connecting-the-dots' enables you to introduce 2 people who can benefit from each other in some way. This is the heart of *PowerNetworking*: adding value to people by introducing them to people who can help them in some way. Clicking the various boxes fills in the 'Identity'. These describe the person by telling 'who they are, what they do, and what they like'.

The actual instructions on installation and operation of *PowerNet* are included in the *Read-me-first.txt* file and in the 'Help' function in the program, as well as in Appendix B.

Computer reporting. *PowerNet* allows you to print various reports. For now, you may just print a phone book sorted however you want. For example, you may only want a book for family members. Or one for business contacts, or alumni, or any combination of these.

The other report is called 'connect-the-dots'. We will cover this in the next Tool.

"Without ambition one starts nothing.
Without work one finishes nothing.
The prize will not be sent to you.
You have to win it.
The man who knows how will always have a job.
The man who also knows why will always be his boss."

- Emerson (1803-1882)

Correctly Working Your Contacts

Now that you have your initial lists of contacts catalogued, it is time to transform your network into a *PowerNetwork*.

Now would be a good time to once again review your S.M.A.R.T. goal:

'Within 2 years, I *will*: create and maintain a *PowerNetwork* of 24 quality people. These people will enable me to succeed in all areas of my life. I will also be an integral part of helping each of these individuals succeed in their efforts. Within this *PowerNetwork*, I will have at least 2 mentors and become a mentor for at least 2.'

At this point you may say, "I have 200 names in my network, that is a lot more than 24." Yes, it is; however, to be a true *PowerNetwork* person, they must meet 2 criteria:

- First, you must add substantial value to their lives in some way.
- Second, they must add substantial value to your life in some way.

The way to transform your contacts into a *PowerNetwork* is to add value to the lives of the people on your list.

Add value to the people on your list.

You cannot have just a give *or* take relationship with people to be a true *PowerNetworker*. It must be a give *and* take relationship. These *PowerNetwork* people are hard to find and valuable beyond belief. However, you must understand that you will need your 200 people on your list in order to find these 24 special people! In fact, you will find that as a *PowerNetworker*, you will have many more than 200 people in your database over the next 2 years. This is excellent. Consider each added name as money in your savings account: an investment that will pay great dividends in your life.

If all this seems a daunting task, let me tell you that it is not. In fact, once you get into the scheme of things, you will find it fun, rewarding, and taking an absolute minimum of your time.

Add value to their lives. Your objective in *PowerNetworking* is to add value to people's lives. You do this by introducing them to people who can help them in some way. You do this by matching people using the 'Identity' section of each form. For example: You have 2 names in your network that have indicated they both love baseball. You know each well and would qualify them as avid baseball fans, perhaps even *rabid* baseball fans. So you call each with a message something like, "George, I know that you are an avid baseball enthusiast. I have a friend named Tom who is also an avid fan. I was wondering if I could introduce the two of you. I have 3 tickets to the next game. I thought the 3 of us could go to the game and I could introduce you to my friend. What do you say?"

Let us assume that both Tom and George go and once they meet, they immediately have common ground. Now, ask yourself the questions:

- "Did you add value to Tom's life by introducing him to George?" The answer is yes.
- "Will Tom and George appreciate my making these introductions?" The answer again is yes.
- "Will Tom and George feel obligated to return the favor to you?" The answer is yes.
- "Will Tom and George look for ways to help you in your efforts." The answer is yes, whenever they can.

Lets take another example: You see that 2 people in your network both work as salesmen in the energy business. Kent, who works in upstream oil production and Rob, who works in downstream oil production. You believe that these people could each benefit by knowing the other. You arrange a meeting. You would call each and say something like, " Kent, I have a friend who is also a salesman in the energy business. Kent, the thought occurred to me that introducing the two of you might help you both. Being in a similar business, you might be able to share leads or contacts. Would you mind meeting for coffee next week?"

Lets say that you made the connection and both Rob and Kent did share leads and contacts, which will benefit them both. Because of your efforts, both increased their businesses. Now, ask yourself the questions:

- "Would Rob and Kent be thankful to you for these introductions?" The answer is yes.
- "Would Rob and Kent feel obligated to you for your efforts?" The answer is yes.
- "Will Rob and Kent be on 'the look out' for ways to help you?" The answer is yes.

I believe you are beginning to see how to 'connect-the-dots' in your network in order to add value to people by introducing them to others in your list.

Another example: You notice in your list of contacts that two of your contacts are both administrative assistants who work for major corporations. You call each and say, "Marsha, I have a friend named Kim who is also an administrative assistant working for a large company. I thought the two of you might do well to know the other. I would like to invite you to meet us after work next Tuesday for coffee. What do you say?"

After the meeting, both Marsha and Kim develop a professional relationship and both benefit from knowing the other. In fact, Kim discovers an opening in her company that Marsha is qualified for. She takes the position, which pays a great deal more than her last job. Now, ask yourself these questions:

- "Would Marsha and Kim be thankful to you for the introductions?" The answer is yes.
- "Would Marsha and Kim feel obligated to you for your efforts?" The answer is yes.
- "Will Marsha and Kim be on 'the look out' for ways to help you?" The answer is yes.

In each of these examples, you were the one to add value to each of these people. Once this was done, a subtle change took place in their psyches. They were endeared to you for your efforts on their behalf. This endearing will cause their subconscious to be 'aware' of you and your efforts. This *awareness* is always there, working in the background.

Why this works...

This awareness has been the topic of psychological studies for quite some time. Psychologists have known that there is a level of activity in the mind that is always working behind the scenes. It is always doing things to protect you, to advance you, to assure you, and often to condemn or reward you.

A small example of how your subconscious works is hearing your name spoken in a noisy room. It is a known fact that you will hear your own name. You will immediately recognize your name being spoken and look to see who spoke it. You will even hear you name if it is below the ambient (average) noise level in the room!

Everyone has experienced this. This is your subconscious working.

When you go out of your way to help some other person, this person's subconscious is aware of this unselfish deed. In addition, this person's subconscious will *actively* be on the lookout for ways to unselfishly help you.

Now, understand that as a *PowerNetworker* you are not looking for this particular person to 'return the favor' (although they well might), you are looking for ways to add value to another person's life, whether they can return the favor or not. What goes around comes around.

Connect-The-Dots. The above examples show how to 'connect-the-dots' in your lists of people. The dots are logical matches of 'who they are', 'what they do', and/or 'what they like'. Some logical examples of connecting dots are:

- People who are involved in the same sport or hobby, such as hunting, fishing, golf, kiting, knitting, reading, etc.
- People who are in the same profession, such as engineers, accountants, technicians, clerical, plumbers, carpenters, mechanics, etc.

- People who are in the same industry, such as petrochemical, banking, home repair, etc.
- People of the same family who may have lost touch over the years. Your accurate database of family members and their addresses is great to share with the rest of the family.

There are also matches that are not immediately obvious. For example, matching people who are in different industries may still have common ground, such as managers in the banking industry and accountants. Both use the services of the other. Or connecting parents with children to a childcare professional. Finding anyone on your list that could benefit from knowing someone else in your network is your goal.

Once you start looking for these 'connect-the-dots' relationships, you will be surprised at how many will jump out at you. Remember, your subconscious will be working behind the scenes to solve the problem you present to it. Once you begin the process, you will find creative ways to match people up.

When to contact your contacts.

Everyone likes to be remembered. The only way they know they are being remembered is to tell them. What better time to remember someone than on his birthday. This is a very special day in each person's life. So, 'when' to contact people is easy. First, always call a person on his birthday. A simple phone call to wish them a happy birthday will make them feel good and make you feel good as well. Cards are nice, but we all like to have the 'high touch' of a phone call to say, "Happy birthday."

When you call someone on his birthday, you are saying something very important to him.   You are saying, "You are important." You are saying, "You are special." You are saying, "I am glad I know you." You are saying, "You are valuable to me as a person and for no other reason."

Consider this, if you call each person on his birthday and wish him a happy birthday, you may be the only person to do so. You never know.

Keeping track of birthdays is a simple matter with the computer program *PowerNet* because it will remind you automatically. If you use a paper system, your job is a little harder, but not much. You will use a calendar, like the one on the following pages, with a blank beside each date. Simply write their names beside their corresponding birthdates.

PowerNet Birthday Reminder

Place the person's name by his birthday and call him on that date.

1-Jan	1-Feb	1-Mar
2-Jan	2-Feb	2-Mar
3-Jan	3-Feb	3-Mar
4-Jan	4-Feb	4-Mar
5-Jan	5-Feb	5-Mar
6-Jan	6-Feb	6-Mar
7-Jan	7-Feb	7-Mar
8-Jan	8-Feb	8-Mar
9-Jan	9-Feb	9-Mar
10-Jan	10-Feb	10-Mar
11-Jan	11-Feb	11-Mar
12-Jan	12-Feb	12-Mar
13-Jan	13-Feb	13-Mar
14-Jan	14-Feb	14-Mar
15-Jan	15-Feb	15-Mar
16-Jan	16-Feb	16-Mar
17-Jan	17-Feb	17-Mar
18-Jan	18-Feb	18-Mar
19-Jan	19-Feb	19-Mar
20-Jan	20-Feb	20-Mar
21-Jan	21-Feb	21-Mar
22-Jan	22-Feb	22-Mar
23-Jan	23-Feb	23-Mar
24-Jan	24-Feb	24-Mar
25-Jan	25-Feb	25-Mar
26-Jan	26-Feb	26-Mar
27-Jan	27-Feb	27-Mar
28-Jan	28-Feb	28-Mar
29-Jan	(29-Feb)	29-Mar
30-Jan		30-Mar
31-Jan		31-Mar

PowerNet Birthday Reminder

Place the person's name by his birthday and call him on that date.

1-Apr	1-May	1-Jun
2-Apr	2-May	2-Jun
3-Apr	3-May	3-Jun
4-Apr	4-May	4-Jun
5-Apr	5-May	5-Jun
6-Apr	6-May	6-Jun
7-Apr	7-May	7-Jun
8-Apr	8-May	8-Jun
9-Apr	9-May	9-Jun
10-Apr	10-May	10-Jun
11-Apr	11-May	11-Jun
12-Apr	12-May	12-Jun
13-Apr	13-May	13-Jun
14-Apr	14-May	14-Jun
15-Apr	15-May	15-Jun
16-Apr	16-May	16-Jun
17-Apr	17-May	17-Jun
18-Apr	18-May	18-Jun
19-Apr	19-May	19-Jun
20-Apr	20-May	20-Jun
21-Apr	21-May	21-Jun
22-Apr	22-May	22-Jun
23-Apr	23-May	23-Jun
24-Apr	24-May	24-Jun
25-Apr	25-May	25-Jun
26-Apr	26-May	26-Jun
27-Apr	27-May	27-Jun
28-Apr	28-May	28-Jun
29-Apr	29-May	29-Jun
30-Apr	30-May	30-Jun
	31-May	

PowerNet Birthday Reminder

Place the person's name by his birthday and call him on that date.

1-Oct	1-Nov	1-Dec
2-Oct	2-Nov	2-Dec
3-Oct	3-Nov	3-Dec
4-Oct	4-Nov	4-Dec
5-Oct	5-Nov	5-Dec
6-Oct	6-Nov	6-Dec
7-Oct	7-Nov	7-Dec
8-Oct	8-Nov	8-Dec
9-Oct	9-Nov	9-Dec
10-Oct	10-Nov	10-Dec
11-Oct	11-Nov	11-Dec
12-Oct	12-Nov	12-Dec
13-Oct	13-Nov	13-Dec
14-Oct	14-Nov	14-Dec
15-Oct	15-Nov	15-Dec
16-Oct	16-Nov	16-Dec
17-Oct	17-Nov	17-Dec
18-Oct	18-Nov	18-Dec
19-Oct	19-Nov	19-Dec
20-Oct	20-Nov	20-Dec
21-Oct	21-Nov	21-Dec
22-Oct	22-Nov	22-Dec
23-Oct	23-Nov	23-Dec
24-Oct	24-Nov	24-Dec
25-Oct	25-Nov	25-Dec
26-Oct	26-Nov	26-Dec
27-Oct	27-Nov	27-Dec
28-Oct	28-Nov	28-Dec
29-Oct	29-Nov	29-Dec
30-Oct	30-Nov	30-Dec
31-Oct		31-Dec

How often? How often do you call them 'just to keep in touch'? To be effective in 'working' your contacts, you should call them at a minimum every 90 days and their birthday; an absolute minimum is yearly. If you use *PowerNet* software, you will be reminded to do this. If you use a paper system to follow up, a calendar system similar to the 'Birthday Reminder' will work as well.

Time requirements. If you think this will be a burden on your time, *think again.* Lets do the math...if you have 228 names on your list, this averages less than one call per day. In fact it averages 5 calls per week. Considering that most calls get answered by an answering machine, it will probably take you about 90 seconds to look up the number, make the call, and leave a brief message. You spend more time than that getting the 5th cup of coffee that you don't need. Remember, this is the type of activity that separates the winners from the losers. Remember: 'The rich get richer, and the poor get poorer...' It is up to you.

Never stop networking... Understand that *PowerNetworkers* never stop networking. They understand that *people* are what really matter in life. They are constantly on the look out for ways to help others because they know that it will be reciprocated... someway, somehow. They never speak with a person that they do not evaluate him to see if he could be someone that they could help.

People Skills Overview

There are some people who can just naturally speak to strangers. They are always comfortable in a strange room full of strange people. They seem to be right at home conversing with total strangers as if they have known them all their lives.

Afraid of meeting people. And then there are people who struggle with meeting new people. They are panicked by the idea of being in a room full of strangers. They want to blend in with the wallpaper so as not to be approached by someone they do not know. The sooner they can leave and get back into their comfort zone, the better they will like it.

Take heart. If you are in the latter group or somewhere in between, take heart. Meeting strangers and being comfortable among strangers requires proper tools and techniques that you CAN learn. If you put into practice what you learn in the next few Tools, you will easily be able to initiate conversations and endear people to you. They will automatically like you and be very much at ease speaking with you. You will also learn how to control the direction of a conversation and how to change the subject completely. You will learn how to include or exclude people who might be standing close to you. You will learn how to qualify people as possible *PowerNetworking* contacts. Your new skills will enable you to meet 'targeted' individuals that can propel your career.

You will learn to systematically become an active listener and utilize the power that 'listening' commands among people.

Defuse the terror. We will defuse the terror some people feel and replace it with courage. You will take 'baby steps' at first, but eventually you will feel confident to go anywhere, and be comfortable in any crowd.

Most importantly, you will actually begin to have fun doing it. You will enjoy making new friends and seeing them feel good about you *because you made them feel good about themselves.*

So, lets put some more Tools in your toolbox that will serve you well in your personal as well as your business life. Remember, it's all about having the right tools and learning how to properly use them. You are about to become a master at using your new 'People Skills' Tools in *PowerNetworking*.

People Skills –
Your Attitude

The next tool in your toolbox is your attitude. Lets talk about attitude. It has been said, "Think you can or think you can't"; both ways, you are correct. Your 'attitude' will determine your success or failure in any endeavor. This includes brushing your teeth or building a house. Your attitude will determine if you do it poorly or greatly.

Importance of Attitude:
"The longer I live, the more I realize the impact of attitude on life. It is more important than the past, than education, than money, than circumstances, than failures, than successes, than what other people think or say or do. It is more important than appearance, giftedness, or skill. It will make or break a company ... a church ... a home. The remarkable thing is we have a choice everyday regarding the *attitude* we will embrace for that day. We cannot change our past ... we cannot change the fact that people will act in a certain way. We cannot change the inevitable. The only thing we can do is play on the one string we have, and that is our *attitude* ... I am convinced that life is 10% what happens to me and 90% how I react to it. And so it is with you ... we are in charge of our *Attitude*."

- Chuck Swindoll, Preacher and author

Your attitude is yours to command. It is not at the mercy of circumstances, health, possessions, money (or lack thereof), education, age, or race. In his book, *Man's Search For Meaning*, Viktor Frankl proved this.

Viktor Frankl was a Jewish medical doctor in Nazi Germany during World War II. He was put into a Nazi death camp along with his family. He had been stripped of all his worldly possessions including his wife and family. He endured the most debauched existence a man can experience including torture, slave labor, and being required to execute fellow Jews in the death camp. At one point he was standing before the Nazis stark naked while they derided him. At this point, he decided that they can take away from him all he possesses including his life, but the one thing they could not take away nor control was his *attitude*. He controlled his *attitude* and no one else did. And if he chose to think positive, if he chose to believe he would live, if he chose to look beyond his situation, the Nazis could do NOTHING ABOUT IT!!!

So what does this mean? It means that you *can* create a positive attitude. You *can* nurture this positive attitude. You *can* prevent circumstances from destroying your positive attitude. You *can* make your positive attitude stronger and doing so will insure your success.

The battle within. Attitude is a battle within your mind; a battle that you can win or lose, depending on which tools you choose to use.

Your mind has voices. Lets talk about your mind. You constantly have voices speaking to you in your mind. For instance, while you are reading these words, the author is speaking to you inside your head. When I count to five, you hear me count. Like this: one, two, three, four, five. You hear me as clearly as if I were speaking to you in person and you heard these numbers with your physical ears. These are the voices that are placed in your mind by reading the printed page.

There are also self-generated voices that are constantly telling you things. Things like:

- "Where did I leave my car keys? You idiot, how many times have you lost your car keys?"
- "You are never going to lose those 15 pounds..."
- "You look so fat..."
- "You really blew it when you did not finish your schooling..."
- "I bet my kids are on drugs..."
- "You can't do that... Who do you think you are?"
- "You are going to fail again."
- "You are not going to get a job. Nobody wants you."
- "You don't have enough education to speak to that person."
- "They are out of your league; they are smarter than you."
- "You are a failure."

- "My boss is going to fire me. I just know I am going to lose my job."
- "He can't do that to me. I'll get back at him."

Sound familiar. Do these voices sound familiar? They should; this is the human condition. 97%+ of all the talk we self-generate is negative. And to compound matters, we speak to ourselves at an astonishing 3000-5000 words a minute! In his excellent book, The Power of Self-Talk, Jim Will PhD opens the door to understanding self-talk and teaches how to control it. This is a life-changing book that is a 'must read'.

You can control your Self-Talk. The amazing thing about your mind is that you can control what it thinks about. Yes, you can... You can control what it says to you. This 'self-talk' is under your control. Lets learn how to determine what your self-talk is saying to you.

Controlling Your Self-Talk

Step #1. Your self-talk is *yours*! Do not glance over this.   This is very important.   The self-talk you constantly listen to is YOURS. It is as much a part of you as your right arm. Like your right arm, you can choose to make it stronger and more useful by exercising it. Or you can ignore it and it will still be there, but most likely it will be of negative import.

Step #2. Learn to recognize when your self-talk becomes negative. When your self-talk begins to be negative, it will often be accompanied by heaviness in your shoulders or arms, a frown on your face, furrowed brows, or a heavy sigh. Your breathing may become shallow. You will most often be looking down and to the right or the left. Be aware of these physical signs and then listen closely to the voices in your head.

Step #3. When you recognize negative self-talk, take control of it. When you evaluate the self-talk as negative, visualize a red flag going up and shout the word 'STOP' as loud as you can.

Why shout the word 'stop'? To answer this question, we will do an experiment:
1. Count to yourself slowly from 1-50.
2. At some point in your counting, speak aloud the your name.

Your counting stopped. If you did this exercise properly, when you spoke your own name aloud, the counting that was taking place in your head stopped!

The voice in your head Stopped!!!

The voices in your head will always stop to listen to what your mouth is saying.

So…. saying out loud the word 'stop' will cause your mind to interrupt the negative self-talk. It is like shouting to your children to divert their attention.

Step #4.   Speak out loud the exact opposite of your negative self-talk. For example: If your self-talk is saying, 'You are a failure,' say out loud,

"Stop!
I am a success,

I am a success,

I am a success!"

Or if the voices are saying, 'You will never get a job,' say out loud:

"Stop!
I will get a job

I will get a job

I *will* get a job!"

Whatever your negative self-talk is saying, speak just the opposite....out loud!

Physical changes to your body.   Your body will manifest some changes when you take control of your self-talk. When you shout the word "stop!" followed by the exact opposite of what the voices are saying, notice how your body stands a little straighter, your head is held a little higher, and you breathe a little deeper. Most importantly, notice how the voices in your head are a little less vocal. The more you practice this, the better you will become. To the point that the voices will not be saying negative phrases, but rather positive phrases that *you have told it to say!!!*   This works and it will free you to succeed.

Caveat. There are some people reading this who have been beaten down by life and overcoming negative self-talk seems an impossible task.   You have been beaten down to the point that you may be comfortable with failure. Failing is a known quantity to you and you have learned how to function in your failures. If this describes you, this technique can turn your life around. It takes courage, constant effort, and a will to change your life for the better. If you can muster the quality decision to take control of your self-talk, you will succeed. Little by little, in small daily steps, but succeed nonetheless. Keep at it. You will free yourself of the negative thoughts that have been weighing you down.

One final note on your self-talk. Be very careful what you 'feed' your mind. Your mind processes everything you feed it. If you watch a constant barrage of negative information, like the evening news, you will be affected by it. If you watch mindless, demeaning programs on television or at the movies, you will be affected by these as well. You would do well to void yourself of all news and negative programming. This includes radio, television, and newspapers. Doing so will free your mind to concentrate on turning your dreams into reality.

Controlling your self-talk will control your attitude. Why is attitude so important? Your attitude determines your every move in life. Not only that, it determines the actions of every person you meet. If you are angry, people will be afraid of you. You know of people you have met who were angry and you were defensive around them. You have also known people who were warm and caring, and you wanted to be around them. You felt comfortable around them. You have met shy people who seemed to have a very poor self-image, and you were uncomfortable around them because they seemed uncomfortable around you.

PowerNetworkers must have a positive attitude. This is not an option. This single quality will determine your success or failure in *PowerNetworking*.

People Skills – Meeting People

Meeting *new* and *wonderful* people. *PowerNetwork*ers are experts at meeting people. People of all kinds. People who are in their same socioeconomic community and people who are out of their socioeconomic community. They are comfortable meeting with the president of the company as well as the mail clerk. They are comfortable speaking with strangers in an elevator or on the street corner. They are at ease with everyone they meet. Young or old, rich or poor. As a *PowerNetworker*, you will be given the tools necessary to interface with anyone, anytime, any place. Be forewarned...it will be fun and rewarding.

The # 1 rule of meeting people and another tool for your toolbox is the knowledge that...

People respond in kind.

What does this mean? **If you are positive,** self-assured, and up beat, <u>they will be, too.</u> If you are frightened, terrified, or afraid, <u>they will be frightened</u>.

If you frown, <u>they will frown</u>. If you have a smile on your face, they will smile. If you are hateful, <u>they will be hateful</u>. If you are aggressive, <u>they will be aggressive</u>. They will respond to you in the same manner in which they are approached.

Use this to your advantage. If people respond in kind, and they do, use this to your advantage. If you want someone to be positive, genuine, and caring...<u>you *first* must be positive, genuine, and caring</u>. The other person will do the same: they will respond in kind.

Make it your objective to be habitually nice. You will want to make being positive, genuine, and caring habitual. You do this by practicing being a pleasant, happy person that children would love to be around. Practice smiling at total strangers with your only motivation being to give them your smile. You will be surprised at how many people will return the smile.

If you are so far removed from this type of activity, go to a park and watch the children playing with their parents. The simple pleasure of watching children at play will bring a smile to your face. This is 'you' responding in kind. People respond in kind.

"There is no friendship, no love, like that of the parent for the child."

-Beecher (1813-1878)
American preacher, orator and writer

Meeting people. OK, now that you have the tools to change your attitudes and the understanding that people respond in kind... lets talk about how to meet people.

People are fascinating.   First, your attitude about people needs to be one of fascination, not fear. Each person is a fascinating individual who has a wealth of interesting experiences no matter who he may be. Each person is interesting in his own way and would love to tell you his story. Why? Because it makes him feel important and appreciated. Everyone has this basic need in his life: to be heard and appreciated. So allow each person you meet the pleasure of being heard and appreciated.

"The deepest principle in human nature is the craving to be appreciated."
-William James (1842-1910)
American Philosopher & Author

How do you do this?
- First, find some way to make a sincere complement.
- Second, make eye contact.
- Third, initiate the 'small talk'.
- Fourth, make him comfortable with you as a person.
- Fifth, ask the questions that allow him to tell his story.

We will discuss each step individually.

Step 1. Make a sincere complement. The first step is to find some way to make a sincere complement. A direct complement will usually cause the person to immediately look into your eyes. Such as,

- "I see by your school ring that you went to the University of Texas... that is an awesome school."
- "That is a beautiful dress you have on. I love the blue and turquoise combination."
- "I could not help but notice your car. It is my dream car."
- "I could not help noticing your lapel pin. It is beautiful."

The idea is to find some physical object that you can complement them on. When they look at you, they most likely will smile and say thank you. *You have just started the process...*

Step 2. Make eye contact to establish trust. It has been written, *"The eyes are the windows of the soul."* The first step in beginning a conversation is to make direct eye contact. Why is this important? We must look into a person's eyes to determine if we can trust them. This is done within seconds. Let the person look into your eyes long enough to determine if you are a threat or not. While they are looking, smile. *Do not look away.*

Why is this important? As children, we lived in a world of giants, all of which could do us harm. Whenever we came in contact with another person, we immediately determined if we could defend ourselves if we had to. We answered the question, "Can I run faster than him?" or "Can I beat him in a fight if I have to?" We did this based on size, first of all. Next, we looked into his eyes to see if he meant us 'harm' or 'good will'. We learned very early in life the difference in the two.

As adults, we never totally lost that 'self defense' mechanism.   We still evaluate people as potential threats by how tall they are and what their eyes tell us. When you initiate contact with a stranger, allow him to look into your eyes to alleviate his ingrained distrust of strangers. When he looks, gently smile and allow him to decide that you really are not a threat. It takes only 2- 3 seconds.

Step 3. Small Talk. After making the initial contact by giving a complement and allowing them to 'look into your eyes', your next step is to start the 'small talk'.

Great Barrier Reef. This is perhaps the greatest barrier for some people. There are some who *freeze up* at the thought of starting a conversation, but it need not be at all frightening. Think of small talk as 'first gear' in the automobile. To start the car rolling, you can always begin by a compliment as in Step 1 above.

Small talk 'generator'. A simple 'small talk' generator is to ask a qualifying question about the object you are admiring.   For example, to expand on the above complements with small talk generators:
- (Ring complement) "What was your major?"
- (Dress complement)   "What color accessories can you wear with that dress?"
- (Car complement) "How quickly can it go from 0 to 60 mph?"

- (Lapel pen complement) "Your lapel pin, is it an antique?"

Generic questions for an event. If you are attending an event, you will want to prepare, in advance, three questions centered on the gathering. For example:
- "What made you decide to come to this event?"
- "How do you know the host?"
- "To what other similar organizations do you belong?"

(Notice that most of these questions require more than one word answers. Try to avoid yes or no questions.)

Their story, not yours. Remember, the objective is to allow *them* the opportunity to tell *their* story, not listen to yours. Once you have asked the question, keep quiet, listen, focus, maintain eye contact, and do not interrupt.

Affirm what they are saying. While the other person is talking, it is very important that you affirm what they are saying. You do this with your eyes, your body language, and affirming phrases. For example, if a person is telling you about the dress she has on, look her in the eye, nod at each complete sentence she says and make a comment that affirms what she has said. For example, you may say:
- "That is a great major. I can tell you really enjoy your career."
- "I can see that the choice of blue and turquoise is one of your favorites."
- "I can now see why you chose that car. What a rush!"

- "Family heirlooms are special because of what they mean, and that obviously means a lot."

Sources of small talk.   Some other small talk generators can come from the covers of 3 magazines: *People, Time,* and *Fortune.*   Having a subscription to each will give you a wealth of information to talk about.

Small talk rules to follow.   Some general rules for small talk are:
- Do not dominate the conversation.
- What *they* have to say is more important than what *you* have to say.
- If they are wrong, keep it to yourself. Do not correct anything they say.
- Do not express an opposite opinion.
- Affirm what they say by repeating it, or nodding as they speak, or validating it by your comments.
- Bring into the conversation as many people as possible.
- Validate who they are as a person by guarding their ego and their self-esteem at all costs, even at the cost of your own ego.
- Remember the two golden phrases "Please" and "thank you."

What NOT to talk about.   Some things to not discuss are:
- Sex
- Politics

- Religion
- Co-workers/bosses
- Weight
- Age
- Sports, if the person is rabid about a particular team.
- Weather (it's boring)
- Illnesses

How to change the topic of a conversation.

As the conversation develops, you may want to change its direction if it is becoming off-color, or unflattering towards someone else or just wandering. This is easily done. First, do not validate the final phrase of the other person by laughing, smiling or commenting. Next, simply pause, then say: "*To change the subject...*" then ask a *feeling* question such as "How do you feel about admissions policy of this organization?"

-or-

"*To change the subject*, how do you feel about changing the meeting to Wednesday?"

-or-

"*To change the subject*, how do you feel about meeting twice a month rather than each week?"

How to exit a conversation

You also need to know how to smoothly exit a conversation. This, too, is a '*change the subject*' type of situation. You can say something such as this, "It has been such a pleasure meeting you. I hope you have a great time at the meeting." Smile, extend your hand, shake hands and leave. Or, if there is a possibility of making a network connection, say, "I am so fortunate to have met you. Thank you for taking the time to speak with me. It is obvious that we have a lot in common. May I call you later to continue our conversation?" Smile, exchange business cards, shake hands and leave.

Don't be rude. A further word about exiting a conversation: it is rude to leave a person alone. It is good manners to leave them speaking with someone else. You can do this by introducing them to someone you have already met. Or if a third party is listening to your conversation, make eye contact with this person while speaking to your new friend. This will function as an invitation to him to join your conversation. With a little practice, this will become very easy.

Joining an existing conversation. To join an existing conversation takes some strategy. First, you don't just barge in. You need to be invited by a word, a look, or a touch. If the person speaking does any of these things, lock onto his eyes and affirm what he is saying by nodding your head in agreement. Look for a chance to make a short validating comment about what he just said, such as, "That is remarkable" or "I am most impressed." Once you have made the comment, you are part of the conversation. It is also a good idea to wait to speak until everyone in the group has spoken and made eye contact with you at least once.

Inviting yourself into the conversation. If there is a large group of people conversing, you can include yourself by a very subtle technique. Stand shoulder square with the group, which will usually be in some sort of circle. Stand where you can make eye contact with each person. Say nothing. Pay close attention to what is being said. Do not take your eyes off the person who is speaking. If a second person starts to speak while the first person is still speaking, do not look at the second person. Continue to look directly at the first person until he finishes his sentence. This act will subconsciously obligate the speaker to you. After you have done this to everyone in the group, when you decide to speak, they will all pay attention to you without interrupting. Doing these things will make you a part of the conversation.

People are most comfortable with people just like themselves. Why is this important? Because when you approach a stranger, he will be more receptive if you are just *like him*. And you can be just like him. How? By a technique called **Pacing.** See Tool #12 for in-depth teaching on this. In brief, Pacing teaches that you take on the same mannerisms, voice patterns, and eye contact as the person to whom you are speaking. For example, if the person, whom you approach, has his right hand in his pocket, you put your right hand in your pocket. If he has his arms crossed, you cross your arms. If he speaks slowly, you speak slowly. If he does not look directly into your eyes except when making a point, you do the same. This is done naturally and evolves slowly during the conversation. The art of *Pacing* puts the other person at ease with you as a stranger.   Why? Because people are most comfortable with themselves and when you start acting and sounding like they do, they are put at ease.   As a *PowerNetworker*, practice pacing with everyone you meet until it becomes a habit.   This will serve you equally well in all your personal conversations as well. It works with strangers as well as old friends, and especially with children.

What people want. One final thought on small talk and meeting strangers.   All people are automatically drawn to 2 things:
- Smiles
- Enthusiasm

Concentrate on smiling. Not with just your mouth but with your eyes, your body, and your movements. Smile from the inside out like you love the world and everyone in it. Next, learn to be enthusiastic about the moment. This is your choice and you can choose to be enthusiastic about anything at any time.   If you have trouble with this, go dancing. Dancing causes the body to move in rhythm with the music and become enthusiastic about the moment. Body movement will automatically generate enthusiasm. So do something that causes your body to move with the idea that this will generate enthusiasm. If all else fails, start singing to yourself and dance to the music and watch how your enthusiasm increases.

"To dance is to smile!"

-Alice Marie Withrow (1947-)
Educator

Where to Network

The answer is "EVERYWHERE!" Wherever there are people, *NETWORK!!!* We live in a world of people. Wherever we go, there are people. Wonderful, fascinating people who are potential *PowerNetworking* contacts. As a *PowerNetworker,* you now have the tools necessary to tap into this unlimited resource.

I once stepped into an elevator. Standing beside me was a man dressed in a business suit and tie. I asked him, "What line of work are you in?"

"I am a buyer for Shell Oil Company," he replied.

"Wow, that must be a fascinating job."

"You might say that."

"What do you purchase for Shell?"

"Currently, I am looking for caustic soda."

"How much are you looking for?

"200,000 metric tons."

"How many boat loads is that?

"About three."

"Well, I just came back from the Orient and may be able to locate just what you need."

"You CAN?! Here is my card, give me a call!"

I could have stepped into the elevator and not said a word and missed doing business with Shell Oil. But I didn't; I took the initiative to look him in the eye, smile, and ask him what he did. You can, too.

So where do you network?   There are 2 types of networking events:

Unplanned

Planned

Unplanned networking opportunities are simply chance meetings. They could be in a park, on a bus, on the subway, at the theater, or anywhere people gather. The unplanned meetings happen when you are among people. Any people. Do not discount these 'chance' meetings. I have met a large number of people for my *PowerNetwork* by 'chance' meetings. The above story is one example.

Planned networking events.   This is when you go to an event with the expressed purpose of networking. When you go to these events, go *with a purpose*. Do your homework. If there is a speaker, find out who will be speaking and read his bio. Make a point of introducing yourself to the speaker at some point. When you do, be prepared to make an informed complement. Ask for his card and ask if you can call or email him with some questions after the event.

If possible, get a list of the board members hosting the event and find out for whom they work. You may need to develop a contact within their companies. If there is a single individual at the event that can help you, *purpose to meet that person.*

> I heard a keynote speaker at a national event and was most impressed by what he had to say. I bought his book and read it with great interest. I found out where he would be speaking next and arranged to get an invitation through one of my *PowerNetwork* contacts. I arrived at the auditorium one hour ahead of time, knowing that all public speakers come early to check the public address system and get an idea of the size of the room. Just as I had predicted, he was there 50 minutes early. I introduced myself and told him how much I had enjoyed his talk in Seattle (informed complement). I also told him that I had read his book and searched for an invitation to this event with the expressed purpose of meeting him and asking him a few questions if he wouldn't mind. That led to a 45-minute one-on-one discussion with the man that was nothing short of awesome.

Notice that in the above story,
- I had a clear objective in mind
- I had done my homework
- I positioned myself physically to allow the 'dream to come true'.

And come true it did.

Networking meetings. If your meeting is a meeting for the expressed purpose of networking, your job just got considerably easier. These meetings are designed to get like-minded individuals together for the purpose of sharing leads and contacts. If you can, get a list of the people who will be there in advance. Pick the few you want especially to meet. At the meeting introduce yourself, exchange business cards, and qualify them as thoroughly as possible. For example, if you were looking for a contact within EXXON USA in the Houston office, you might ask, "I see you work with EXXON; *I need your help.* I am trying to get an introduction to the head of purchasing for professional services within EXXON. Can you help me?" He will most likely be able to help in some capacity. You would then follow up by asking what he does for EXXON and if he wants to accomplish anything with which you may be able to assist him. **Remember the heart of *PowerNetworking* is helping others.** You would then ask if you might call him later to discuss either issue. While on the call, you would fill out your *PowerNetwor*king form (Figure 20A).

Meet the leaders. A few select individuals always run meetings such as these. Get close to these people and volunteer to help in their efforts. Helping them will get you to the top of the 'food chain' and allow you access to the 'who's who' that can help you.

Closing Comments

You now have all the tools you need. You are totally equipped with a toolbox full of all the tools you need to make it in this world.

- You know the absolute power of the telephone and how to use it to find decision makers and get appointments.
- You have the skills necessary to interview like a professional and distinguish yourself in front of people so that they are endeared to you as a person.
- You have the people skills necessary to meet people and make them comfortable around you and build a dynamic *PowerNetwork*.

You are set. The rest is up to you. It always has been and it always will be up to you. You have what it takes and you now have the tools to make it happen. And happen it will. How do I know? Because you are reading this book, and people like you are driven to make yourself and those around you better. I am honored to have served you by teaching you what I know.

If you liked this book, I have produced 3 complementary training videos that cover each of these topics as well:

- Using the Phone in Your Job Search
- Interview Like a Professional
- *PowerNetworking,* the 'New' Job Security

Each of these videos is designed to run on your PC or a modern DVD. Order forms are in the back of this book.

I am also available for group workshops or for motivational speaking engagements. For additional details please go to my website, www.GetAJob.ws, or call me at 281-481-6996.

I would enjoy doing anything I can to help you *Get A Job...NOW!!!* Best wishes for a prosperous and happy future.

List of Emotions

Emotion or Passion: An affective state of consciousness, often accompanied by physiological changes (as joy, sorrow, fear, and hate), to be distinguished from cognitive (knowledge and perception) and volitional (willing and intending) states of consciousness [Dictionary definition]. According to *Cognitive Theories of Emotions*, an emotion can have a cognitive component, a judgment. Such cognitive theories go back to Aristotle and the Stoics, not to be confused with a bodily appetite, as hunger or thirst.

Mood: A disposition to acquire certain emotional states of mind in certain situations. For instance, depression is a mood that weakens one's ability to become easily elated or sad.

acceptance	anger	ashamed
adoration	annoyed	astonished
affection	anticipation	attraction
agitated	anxiousness	awed
Alert	appreciative	
amazed	apprehensive	bewildered
ambition	ardent	bitter
amused	aroused	bliss

blue
boastful
bored
breathless
bubbly

calamitous
calm
camaraderie
cautious
cheerful
cocky
cold
collected
comfortable
compassionate
concerned
confident
confused
contempt
content
courageous
cowardly
crafty
crazy
cruelty
crummy
crushed
curious
cynic

dark
dejected
delighted
delirious
denial

depression
desire
despair
determined
detest
devastated
disappointed
discouraged
disgust
disheartened
dismal
dispirited
distracted
distressed
dopey
down
dreadful
dreary

eager
ecstatic
embarrassed
emotional
emphatic
emptiness
enchanted
enigmatic
enraged
enthusiastic
envy
euphoric
excited
exhausted
expectation
exuberance

fascinated
fear
flabbergasted
fight-or-flight
foolish
frazzled
frustrated
fulfillment
furious

gay
giddy
gleeful
gloomy
goofy
grateful
gratified
greedy
grief
grouchy
grudging
guilty
happy
hate
heartbroken
homesick
hopeful
hopeless
horrified
hostile
humiliated
humored
hurt
hyper
hysterical

indignation
infatuation
infuriated
inner peace
innocent
insanity
insecure
insecure
inspired
interest
intimidated
invidious
irate
irritability
irritated

jaded
jealousy
joy

kind

lazy
left out
liberated
lively
loathsome
lonely
longing
love
lovesick
loyal
lust

mad
mean
melancholic
mellow
mercy
merry
miserable
morbid
mourning

needed
needy
nervous

obscene
obsessed
offended
optimistic
outraged
overwhelmed

pacified
pain
panicky
paranoia
passion
pathetic
peaceful
perturbation
pessimistic
petrified
pity
playful
pleased
pleasure

possessive
pride
proud
puzzled

rage
relief
remorse
resentment
resignation
resolved

sadness
scared
scorn
selfish
sensual
sexy
shame
sheepish
shocked
shy
sincerity
solemn
somber
sorrow
sorry
spirited
stressed
strong
superior
surprised
sweet
sympathetic

temperamental

terrified

threatened

thrilled

tired

tranquil

troubled

trust

uncertainty

uneasiness

unhappy

upset

vengeful

vicious

warm

weary

worn-out

worried

worthless

yearning

How to Create a Personal Bio

A personal bio is a short (15-20 second) explanation of who you are, what you do and what you are looking for. Think of your personal bio as your 'commercial'. It is what you would tell a stranger if you met one in an elevator. You only have 20 seconds and your "bio" is what you would tell them. The purpose is to tell them who you are, what you do, and what you are looking for.

To be effective, you must devote your bio to writing. This will enable you to 'fine tune' your story. When completed, you will then memorize your bio so that you can easily tell anyone at anytime. When you tell them your bio, look them in the eye until your bio is complete. Doing so will cause them to focus on what you are saying and consequently have a greater impact.

Some simple guidelines for the creation of your personal bio are:
- Use short declarative sentences of 17 words or less.
- Incorporate numbers to add strength.
- State what type of position you are seeking.

Samples of a few bios are on the next page.

"I am a certified project manager. I have 22 years experience in major projects in the oil and gas, medical, and banking industries.   My projects include technology, ground-up commercial construction, back fill construction, and security. I am currently looking for a position in project management."

"I am an administrative assistant with 12 years experience. I have worked in both large corporations and small family owned establishments. My forte lies in my ability to 'second guess' my boss so as to keep him productive. I also have experience in arranging large meetings with vendors and customers. I am looking for another administrative assistant position."

"I am a recent graduate looking for my first permanent job. My skills include metalworking, computer aided design, and operating a 36-inch computer controlled turret lathe. I am willing to travel and hope to work in the petrochemical industry or the medical field."

"I have 10 years experience as an outside sales person responsible for major clients. My territory covered 2 states and generated $11 million per year in the industrial components industry. I am looking for a manufacturer's rep position or would work directly for a local manufacturer."

"I am a housewife who is transitioning back into the workforce. I have worked in manufacturing and office support before raising my 3 children. I am looking for a position as electronic assembler or office clerk."

PowerNet Software Instructions

This book comes with a single user copy of *PowerNet* software. The following is a reprint of the 'Readme-first' which gives detailed instructions on the installation of the software on a PC running Microsoft Windows 95 or greater. As indicated, *PLEASE* read these instructions carefully before you start.

PowerNet Installation

READ THESE INSTRUCTIONS <u>COMPLETELY</u> BEFORE BEGINNING THE INSTALLATION PROCESS!!

For most users, the installation of *PowerNet* will be a simple one step process. It is suggested that you attempt the simple process first. The installation procedure will tell you if anything else is needed.

There are 6 files in the software directory of the CD - one of them is this <u>readme-first</u> file. So if you are reading this, I know you have found the software. You should see the following files:

readme-first.rft
Setup.exe

PowerNet.msi
dotnetfx.exe
Setup.ini
MDAC_TYP.exe

Simple Install

To invoke the simple installation you will double-click on Setup.exe - this will lead you through the installation of *PowerNet*. When installation is complete the program will be installed where you requested it (the default installation directory is preferred), a desktop icon will be created and *PowerNet* will be listed in your programs list on the **start** menu.

DotNet Framework/Environment Install

PowerNet requires the DotNet execution framework. Most Windows XP and Windows ME systems will have the DotNet framework already installed. IF IT IS NOT INSTALLED, you will get a message during the installation attempted above telling you that you need the DotNet framework or environment. It will tell you to go online to get it - but you don't have to do that. **The DotNet framework is on this CD**. Simply double-click the file **dotnetfc.exe** and the DotNet framework will be installed. When the installation of the dotnetfx.exe is complete, return to the previous paragraph to do the Simple Install.

Microsoft Data Access Components

PowerNet requires version 2.7 or later of the Microsoft Data Access Components (MDAC). You will know if your MDAC version is a problem when you run *PowerNet* for the first time.   If you do not get a message telling you there is a problem, then you have a version that is acceptable. **If you do get such a message you will need to install the**

MDAC_TYP.exe file on the CD. Simply click on **MDAC_TYP.exe.** It will self-install. After installing the MDAC upgrade simply invoke *PowerNet* again via the icon on your desktop and you should be up and running.

If you have problems not addressed here, email problem to: powernet@smallstuff.org

Bibliography

Bolles, Richard D. *What Color is Your Parachute? 2000.*
Berkeley, California: Ten Speed Press, 2000.

Boothman, Nicholas. *How to Make People Like You in 90
Seconds or Less.* New York: Workman Publishing,
2000.

Carnegie, Dale. *How to Win Friends and Influence People.*
New York: Pocket Books, 1998.

Covey, Stephen. *7 Habits of Highly Effective People:
Restoring the Character Ethic.* New York: Free Press,
2004

Frankl, Viktor Emil. *Man's Search for Meaning.* Boston:
Beacon Press, 2000.

Lassiter, Pam. *The New Job Security – Five Strategies to
Take Control of Your Career.* Berkeley, California:
Ten Speed Press, 2002.

Molloy, John. *The New Women's Dress for Success.* New
York: Warner Books, 1996.

Sabath, Ann Marie. *Beyond Business Casual: What to
Wear to Work if You Want to Get Ahead.* Franklin
Lakes, N.J.: Career Press, 2000.

Bibliography

Seuss, Dr. *Green Eggs and Ham*. New York: Random House, 1960.

Sher, Barbara. *I Could Do Anything If I Only Knew What It Was – How to Discover What You Really Want and How to Get it*. New York: Dell Publishing, 1994.

Watts, Duncan J. *6 Degrees – The Science of a Connected Age*. New York: W. W. Norton & Company, Inc., 2003.

Will, Phil Ph.D. *The Power of Self-Talk*. Houston, Texas: Oxford-Hanover Publisher, 2005.

Will, Phil Ph.D. *The Image Analysis Workbook*. Houston, Texas: Oxford-Hanover Publisher, 2005.

Get A Job...NOW!!!
Training Videos

SOAR Publishing also offers this powerful training in a video series. The *Get A Job...NOW!!!* videos are designed to play on a standard PC or modern DVD player. These are invaluable tools for your job search.

- Using The Phone In Your Job Search
- Interview Like a Professional
- PowerNetworking...the 'New' Job Security

SPECIAL!!! Order all 3 and save 10%!!! Plus includes binder.

Quick Order Form

Online orders: www.GetAJob.ws
Fax orders: 281-481-6137
Telephone orders: 281-481-6996 or 888-333-2021 toll free for TX and LA only.
Postal orders: S O A R Publishing, 10523 Sagecanyon Dr., Houston, TX 77089

Qty.	Item	Price	Total
[ ]	Using the Phone Video	$39.95	$_____.___
[ ]	Interviewing Video	$39.95	$_____.___
[ ]	Networking Video	$39.95	$_____.___
[ ]	SPECIAL – 3 video sets with binder	$110.00	$_____.___
[ ]	*Get A Job...Now!!!* Book	$24.95	$_____.___
[ ]	*Get A Job...Now!!!* AudioBook	$24.95	$_____.___
	TOTAL		$_____.___

Sales Tax: Texas residents, add 8.25%.
Shipping: Single CD sets $1.50 each; SPECIAL $7.00 set; book/audio book $5.00 each; International orders, add $5.00

Payment: [ ]Check   [ ]Credit Card
[ ]Visa,[ ]Mastercard,[ ]American Express,[ ]Discover
Card Number:_____
Expiration Date:_____/_____
Name on Card:_____
Billing Address:_____
_____
Mailing Address, if different:_____
_____

www.GetAJob.ws

Fold here

S O A R Publishing
10523 Sagecanyon Dr.
Houston, TX 77089

Fold here

Quick Order Form

Online orders: www.GetAJob.ws
Fax orders: 281-481-6137
Telephone orders: 281-481-6996 or 888-333-2021 toll free for TX and LA only.
Postal orders: S O A R Publishing, 10523 Sagecanyon Dr., Houston, TX 77089

Qty.	Item	Price	Total
[ ]	Using the Phone Video	$39.95	$_____.____
[ ]	Interviewing Video	$39.95	$_____.____
[ ]	Networking Video	$39.95	$_____.____
[ ]	SPECIAL – 3 video sets with binder	$110.00	$_____.____
[ ]	*Get A Job...Now!!!* Book	$24.95	$_____.____
[ ]	*Get A Job...Now!!!* AudioBook	$24.95	$_____.____
	TOTAL		$_____.____

Sales Tax: Texas residents, add 8.25%.
Shipping: Single CD sets $1.50 each; SPECIAL $7.00 set; book/audio book $5.00 each; International orders, add $5.00
Payment: [ ]Check   [ ]Credit Card
[ ]Visa,[ ]Mastercard,[ ]American Express,[ ]Discover
Card Number:_____
Expiration Date:_____/_____
Name on Card:_____
Billing Address:_____
_____
Mailing Address, if different:_____
_____

www.GetAJob.ws

Fold here

S O A R Publishing
10523 Sagecanyon Dr.
Houston, TX 77089

Fold here